MW01518806

Aroma Freedom Technique Session & Affirmation Pocket Journal

For Beginning AFT Users

~ a companion to the book
The Aroma Freedom Technique

26 Sessions

created by Angie Taylor
Certified Aroma Freedom Technique Practitioner

Connect on Facebook at www.Facebook.com/EmotionOilWellness

You may reach Angie Taylor at
www.EmotionOilWellness.com or angie@emotionoilwellness.com

ISBN: 9781090797919

I love that life is a journey! More importantly it's a never ending adventure that takes us through twists and turns that stretch us further than we ever imagined. The things we have the opportunity to learn about ourselves on a daily basis is truly inspiring and, for far too many, frightening.

Aroma Freedom Technique, created by Dr. Benjamin Perkus, gives us all a way to truly enjoy the journey and look forward to every adventure that life throws our way. Using essential oils to quickly release limiting beliefs that have a root in past emotional events gives each one of us the real gift of unleashing the God-given purpose we have held deep inside since our moment of birth.

I created this *Aroma Freedom Technique* (AFT) *Session & Affirmation Journal* so you have a place to keep track of your journey and adventures. The very first page is where you can keep a running list of things you want to work on as it's highly satisfying to check off what we have accomplished. The remaining pages are for you to use as you take yourself through an AFT session followed by the affirmation and daily anchoring routine. When you're ready to move forward, simply turn the page and begin to fill in each area.

Always remember that there is a growing list of Certified AFT Practitioners at **www.AromaFreedom.com** in case you get stuck and need some guidance. We are here to support you along your journey and be your guide as you move through the adventures on which your life's path takes you.

Are you ready to start your journey? Hang on for the adventure of a lifetime!!

Angie Taylor

Angie Taylor
Certified AFT Practitioner
Certified AFT Instructor

What I Want in Life

_____

_____

_____

_____

_____

_____

_____

_____

_____

_____

_____

_____

_____

_____

_____

_____

_____

_____

_____

_____

_____

_____

_____

_____

_____

_____

_____

_____

_____

Date of Personal AFT Session: _____

[ROUND 1] Step 1 - Set Your Intention/Goal: _____

_____

_____

Rate your intention/goal. How possible does it feel? (Circle One)

Zero Hope - 0 1 2 3 4 5 6 7 8 9 10 - Absolute Confidence

Step 2 - What does the negative voice say that tells you this is not possible? _____

_____

Step 3 - How do you feel when you hear this negative voice (find ONE word)? _____

Step 4 - Where do you feel this emotion in your body? _____

_____

Step 5 - Drift back to an earlier time when you felt the same way - same emotion in the same place in your body. This memory may appear as a single image or a series of memories, like a movie. You might also have nothing come up. Any of these are okay. Notes on previous memory _____

_____

_____

Step 6 - Smell Memory Release Blend (equal parts YL Lavender, YL Frankincense and YL Stress Away) or other oils - specify which oils used: _____

Step 7 - Notice changes to memory, emotion, bodily sensation: _____

_____

_____

Step 8 - Is there a new belief or mindset that has emerged? _____

_____

_____

Step 9 - Read the original intention/goal and rate it again - how possible does it feel now? (circle one)

Zero Hope - 0 1 2 3 4 5 6 7 8 9 10 - Absolute Confidence

(If 8 or higher (or if no negative voice), skip to Step 10 - the Affirmation. If less than 8, return to Step 2 on next page.)

How far have you shifted thus far?

Starting Number: _____ New Number: _____

[ROUND 2] Step 2 - What does the inner voice say that tells you this is not possible? _____

_____

Step 3 - How do you feel when you hear this inner voice (find ONE word)? _____

Step 4 - Where do you feel this emotion in your body? _____

_____

Step 5 - Drift back to an earlier time when you felt the same way - same emotion in the same place in your body. This memory may appear as a single image or a series of memories, like a movie. You might also have nothing come up. Any of these are okay. Notes on previous memory _____

_____

_____

Step 6 - Smell YL Inner Child blend or other oils - specify which oils used:

_____

Step 7 - Notice changes to memory, emotion, bodily sensation: _____

_____

_____

Step 8 - Is there a new belief or mindset that has emerged? _____

_____

_____

Step 9 - Read the original intention/goal and rate it again - how possible does it feel now? (circle one)

Zero Hope - 0 1 2 3 4 5 6 7 8 9 10 - Absolute Confidence

(If 8 or higher (or if no negative voice), skip to Step 10 - the Affirmation. If less than 8, return to Step 2 on next page.)

Look how far you've shifted!

Starting Number: _____ Second Number: _____
Third Number: _____

6

[ROUND 3] Step 2 - What does the inner voice say that tells you this is not possible? _____

Step 3 - How do you feel when you hear this inner voice (find ONE word)? _____

Step 4 - Where do you feel this emotion in your body? _____

Step 5 - Drift back to an earlier time when you felt the same way - same emotion in the same place in your body. This memory may appear as a single image or a series of memories, like a movie. You might also have nothing come up. Any of these are okay. Notes on previous memory _____

_____

Step 6 - Smell YL Release blend or other oils - specify which oils used:

_____

Step 7 - Notice changes to memory, emotion, bodily sensation: _____

_____

Step 8 - Is there a new belief or mindset that has emerged? _____

_____

Step 9 - Read the original intention/goal and rate it again - how possible does it feel now? (circle one)

Zero Hope - 0 1 2 3 4 5 6 7 8 9 10 - Absolute Confidence

Look how far you've shifted!

Starting Number: _____ Second Number: _____
Third Number: _____ Final Number: _____

(Time to set your affirmation, even if you're not yet at an 8 or higher. More shifting will occur during the next 3 steps.)

Step 10 - Affirmation: _____

_____

_____

Step 11 - Stand in Power Pose: Repeat the affirmation for 2 minutes, twice daily, with conviction while standing in a power pose. Smell *Believe™* or *Transformation™* Oil Blend as you do this. (You may choose another transforming oil if you'd like, such as *Build Your Dream™*, *Magnify Your Purpose™*, etc) Chosen Oil & Pose: _____

Repeat for *at least three consecutive days,* or until you create a new affirmation. Check off each box when complete.

Always make sure that your energy feels clear when you say the statement. If you experience inner resistance, use the AFT process to identify and release any negative thoughts, feelings, or memories that come up.

Date	AM	PM

Step 12 - Make Your Plan of Action: _____

_____

_____

_____

_____

_____

Follow-up - What has changed in your life because of THIS Aroma Freedom Technique Session? _____

_____

_____

_____

_____

Program your mind daily! As soon as one affirmation is complete or the goal has been reached, create another. Make affirmations a daily habit and soon you will not feel right unless you have done your daily practice. This will keep you focused in the direction of your dreams. Feel free to experiment with different oils as you progress.

Date of Personal AFT Session: _____

[ROUND 1] Step 1 - Set Your Intention/Goal: _____

_____

_____

Rate your intention/goal. How possible does it feel? (Circle One)

Zero Hope - 0 1 2 3 4 5 6 7 8 9 10 - Absolute Confidence

Step 2 - What does the negative voice say that tells you this is not possible? _____

_____

Step 3 - How do you feel when you hear this negative voice (find ONE word)? _____

Step 4 - Where do you feel this emotion in your body? _____

_____

Step 5 - Drift back to an earlier time when you felt the same way - same emotion in the same place in your body. This memory may appear as a single image or a series of memories, like a movie. You might also have nothing come up. Any of these are okay. Notes on previous memory _____

_____

_____

Step 6 - Smell Memory Release Blend (equal parts YL Lavender, YL Frankincense and YL Stress Away) or other oils - specify which oils used: _____

Step 7 - Notice changes to memory, emotion, bodily sensation: _____

_____

_____

Step 8 - Is there a new belief or mindset that has emerged? _____

_____

_____

Step 9 - Read the original intention/goal and rate it again - how possible does it feel now? (circle one)

Zero Hope - 0 1 2 3 4 5 6 7 8 9 10 - Absolute Confidence

(If 8 or higher (or if no negative voice), skip to Step 10 - the Affirmation. If less than 8, return to Step 2 on next page.)

How far have you shifted thus far?

Starting Number: _____ New Number: _____

[ROUND 2] Step 2 - What does the inner voice say that tells you this is not possible? _____

Step 3 - How do you feel when you hear this inner voice (find ONE word)? _____
Step 4 - Where do you feel this emotion in your body? _____

Step 5 - Drift back to an earlier time when you felt the same way - same emotion in the same place in your body. This memory may appear as a single image or a series of memories, like a movie. You might also have nothing come up. Any of these are okay. Notes on previous memory _____

_____

Step 6 - Smell YL Inner Child blend or other oils - specify which oils used:

_____

Step 7 - Notice changes to memory, emotion, bodily sensation: _____

_____

Step 8 - Is there a new belief or mindset that has emerged? _____

_____

Step 9 - Read the original intention/goal and rate it again - how possible does it feel now? (circle one)

Zero Hope - 0 1 2 3 4 5 6 7 8 9 10 - Absolute Confidence

(If 8 or higher (or if no negative voice), skip to Step 10 - the Affirmation. If less than 8, return to Step 2 on next page.)

Look how far you've shifted!

Starting Number: _____ Second Number: _____
Third Number: _____

[ROUND 3] Step 2 - What does the inner voice say that tells you this is not possible? _____

Step 3 - How do you feel when you hear this inner voice (find ONE word)? _____

Step 4 - Where do you feel this emotion in your body? _____

Step 5 - Drift back to an earlier time when you felt the same way - same emotion in the same place in your body. This memory may appear as a single image or a series of memories, like a movie. You might also have nothing come up. Any of these are okay. Notes on previous memory _____

_____

Step 6 - Smell YL Release blend or other oils - specify which oils used:

_____

Step 7 - Notice changes to memory, emotion, bodily sensation: _____

_____

Step 8 - Is there a new belief or mindset that has emerged? _____

_____

Step 9 - Read the original intention/goal and rate it again - how possible does it feel now? (circle one)

Zero Hope - 0 1 2 3 4 5 6 7 8 9 10 - Absolute Confidence

Look how far you've shifted!

Starting Number: _____ Second Number: _____
Third Number: _____ Final Number: _____

(Time to set your affirmation, even if you're not yet at an 8 or higher. More shifting will occur during the next 3 steps.)

Step 10 - Affirmation: _____

_____

_____

Step 11 - Stand in Power Pose: Repeat the affirmation for 2 minutes, twice daily, with conviction while standing in a power pose. Smell *Believe™* or *Transformation™* Oil Blend as you do this. (You may choose another transforming oil if you'd like, such as *Build Your Dream™*, *Magnify Your Purpose™*, etc) Chosen Oil & Pose: _____

Repeat for *at least three consecutive days*, or until you create a new affirmation. Check off each box when complete.

Always make sure that your energy feels clear when you say the statement. If you experience inner resistance, use the AFT process to identify and release any negative thoughts, feelings, or memories that come up.

Date	AM	PM

Step 12 - Make Your Plan of Action: _____

_____

_____

_____

_____

_____

Follow-up - What has changed in your life because of THIS Aroma Freedom Technique Session? _____

_____

_____

_____

_____

Program your mind daily! As soon as one affirmation is complete or the goal has been reached, create another. Make affirmations a daily habit and soon you will not feel right unless you have done your daily practice. This will keep you focused in the direction of your dreams. Feel free to experiment with different oils as you progress.

Date of Personal AFT Session: _____

[ROUND 1] Step 1 - Set Your Intention/Goal: _____

_____

Rate your intention/goal. How possible does it feel? (Circle One)

Zero Hope - 0 1 2 3 4 5 6 7 8 9 10 - Absolute Confidence

Step 2 - What does the negative voice say that tells you this is not possible? _____

_____

Step 3 - How do you feel when you hear this negative voice (find ONE word)? _____

Step 4 - Where do you feel this emotion in your body? _____

_____

Step 5 - Drift back to an earlier time when you felt the same way - same emotion in the same place in your body. This memory may appear as a single image or a series of memories, like a movie. You might also have nothing come up. Any of these are okay. Notes on previous memory ____

_____

Step 6 - Smell Memory Release Blend (equal parts YL Lavender, YL Frankincense and YL Stress Away) or other oils - specify which oils used: _____

Step 7 - Notice changes to memory, emotion, bodily sensation: _____

_____

Step 8 - Is there a new belief or mindset that has emerged? _____

_____

Step 9 - Read the original intention/goal and rate it again - how possible does it feel now? (circle one)

Zero Hope - 0 1 2 3 4 5 6 7 8 9 10 - Absolute Confidence

(If 8 or higher (or if no negative voice), skip to Step 10 - the Affirmation. If less than 8, return to Step 2 on next page.)

13

How far have you shifted thus far?

Starting Number: _____ New Number: _____

[ROUND 2] Step 2 - What does the inner voice say that tells you this is not possible? _____

Step 3 - How do you feel when you hear this inner voice (find ONE word)? _____

Step 4 - Where do you feel this emotion in your body? _____

Step 5 - Drift back to an earlier time when you felt the same way - same emotion in the same place in your body. This memory may appear as a single image or a series of memories, like a movie. You might also have nothing come up. Any of these are okay. Notes on previous memory _____

_____
_____

Step 6 - Smell YL Inner Child blend or other oils - specify which oils used:

_____

Step 7 - Notice changes to memory, emotion, bodily sensation: _____

_____

Step 8 - Is there a new belief or mindset that has emerged? _____

_____

Step 9 - Read the original intention/goal and rate it again - how possible does it feel now? (circle one)

Zero Hope - 0 1 2 3 4 5 6 7 8 9 10 - Absolute Confidence

(If 8 or higher (or if no negative voice), skip to Step 10 - the Affirmation. If less than 8, return to Step 2 on next page.)

Look how far you've shifted!

Starting Number: _____ Second Number: _____
Third Number: _____

[ROUND 3] Step 2 - What does the inner voice say that tells you this is not possible? _____

_____

Step 3 - How do you feel when you hear this inner voice (find ONE word)? _____

Step 4 - Where do you feel this emotion in your body? _____

_____

Step 5 - Drift back to an earlier time when you felt the same way - same emotion in the same place in your body. This memory may appear as a single image or a series of memories, like a movie. You might also have nothing come up. Any of these are okay. Notes on previous memory _____

_____

Step 6 - Smell YL Release blend or other oils - specify which oils used:

_____

Step 7 - Notice changes to memory, emotion, bodily sensation: _____

_____

Step 8 - Is there a new belief or mindset that has emerged? _____

_____

Step 9 - Read the original intention/goal and rate it again - how possible does it feel now? (circle one)

Zero Hope - 0 1 2 3 4 5 6 7 8 9 10 - Absolute Confidence

Look how far you've shifted!

Starting Number: _____ Second Number: _____
Third Number: _____ Final Number: _____

(Time to set your affirmation, even if you're not yet at an 8 or higher. More shifting will occur during the next 3 steps.)

Step 10 - Affirmation: _____

_____

_____

Step 11 - Stand in Power Pose: Repeat the affirmation for 2 minutes, twice daily, with conviction while standing in a power pose. Smell *Believe™* or *Transformation™* Oil Blend as you do this. (You may choose another transforming oil if you'd like, such as *Build Your Dream™*, *Magnify Your Purpose™*, etc) Chosen Oil & Pose: _____

Repeat for *at least three consecutive days*, or until you create a new affirmation. Check off each box when complete.

Always make sure that your energy feels clear when you say the statement. If you experience inner resistance, use the AFT process to identify and release any negative thoughts, feelings, or memories that come up.

Date	AM	PM

Step 12 - Make Your Plan of Action: _____

_____

_____

_____

_____

_____

Follow-up - What has changed in your life because of THIS Aroma Freedom Technique Session? _____

_____

_____

_____

_____

Program your mind daily! As soon as one affirmation is complete or the goal has been reached, create another. Make affirmations a daily habit and soon you will not feel right unless you have done your daily practice. This will keep you focused in the direction of your dreams. Feel free to experiment with different oils as you progress.

16

Date of Personal AFT Session: _____

[ROUND 1] Step 1 - Set Your Intention/Goal: _____

_____

_____

Rate your intention/goal. How possible does it feel? (Circle One)

Zero Hope - 0 1 2 3 4 5 6 7 8 9 10 - Absolute Confidence

Step 2 - What does the negative voice say that tells you this is not possible? _____

_____

Step 3 - How do you feel when you hear this negative voice (find ONE word)? _____

Step 4 - Where do you feel this emotion in your body? _____

_____

Step 5 - Drift back to an earlier time when you felt the same way - same emotion in the same place in your body. This memory may appear as a single image or a series of memories, like a movie. You might also have nothing come up. Any of these are okay. Notes on previous memory _____

_____

_____

Step 6 - Smell Memory Release Blend (equal parts YL Lavender, YL Frankincense and YL Stress Away) or other oils - specify which oils used: _____

Step 7 - Notice changes to memory, emotion, bodily sensation: _____

_____

_____

Step 8 - Is there a new belief or mindset that has emerged? _____

_____

Step 9 - Read the original intention/goal and rate it again - how possible does it feel now? (circle one)

Zero Hope - 0 1 2 3 4 5 6 7 8 9 10 - Absolute Confidence

(If 8 or higher (or if no negative voice), skip to Step 10 - the Affirmation. If less than 8, return to Step 2 on next page.)

How far have you shifted thus far?

Starting Number: _____ New Number: _____

[ROUND 2] Step 2 - What does the inner voice say that tells you this is not possible? _____

Step 3 - How do you feel when you hear this inner voice (find ONE word? _____

Step 4 - Where do you feel this emotion in your body? _____

Step 5 - Drift back to an earlier time when you felt the same way - same emotion in the same place in your body. This memory may appear as a single image or a series of memories, like a movie. You might also have nothing come up. Any of these are okay. Notes on previous memory _____

_____

Step 6 - Smell YL Inner Child blend or other oils - specify which oils used:

_____

Step 7 - Notice changes to memory, emotion, bodily sensation: _____

_____

Step 8 - Is there a new belief or mindset that has emerged? _____

_____

Step 9 - Read the original intention/goal and rate it again - how possible does it feel now? (circle one)

Zero Hope - 0 1 2 3 4 5 6 7 8 9 10 - Absolute Confidence

(If 8 or higher (or if no negative voice), skip to Step 10 - the Affirmation. If less than 8, return to Step 2 on next page.)

Look how far you've shifted!

Starting Number: _____ Second Number: _____
Third Number: _____

[ROUND 3] Step 2 - What does the inner voice say that tells you this is not possible? _____

Step 3 - How do you feel when you hear this inner voice (find ONE word)? _____

Step 4 - Where do you feel this emotion in your body? _____

Step 5 - Drift back to an earlier time when you felt the same way - same emotion in the same place in your body. This memory may appear as a single image or a series of memories, like a movie. You might also have nothing come up. Any of these are okay. Notes on previous memory _____
_____

Step 6 - Smell YL Release blend or other oils - specify which oils used:
_____

Step 7 - Notice changes to memory, emotion, bodily sensation: _____
_____

Step 8 - Is there a new belief or mindset that has emerged? _____
_____

Step 9 - Read the original intention/goal and rate it again - how possible does it feel now? (circle one)

Zero Hope - 0 1 2 3 4 5 6 7 8 9 10 - Absolute Confidence

Look how far you've shifted!

Starting Number: _____ Second Number: _____
Third Number: _____ Final Number: _____

(Time to set your affirmation, even if you're not yet at an 8 or higher. More shifting will occur during the next 3 steps.)

Step 10 - Affirmation: _____
_____
_____

Step 11 - Stand in Power Pose: Repeat the affirmation for 2 minutes, twice daily, with conviction while standing in a power pose. Smell *Believe*™ or *Transformation*™ Oil Blend as you do this. (You may choose another transforming oil if you'd like, such as *Build Your Dream*™, *Magnify Your Purpose*™, etc) Chosen Oil & Pose: _____

Repeat for *at least three consecutive days*, or until you create a new affirmation. Check off each box when complete.

Always make sure that your energy feels clear when you say the statement. If you experience inner resistance, use the AFT process to identify and release any negative thoughts, feelings, or memories that come up.

Date	AM	PM

Step 12 - Make Your Plan of Action: _____

_____

_____

_____

_____

_____

Follow-up - What has changed in your life because of THIS Aroma Freedom Technique Session? _____

_____

_____

_____

_____

Program your mind daily! As soon as one affirmation is complete or the goal has been reached, create another. Make affirmations a daily habit and soon you will not feel right unless you have done your daily practice. This will keep you focused in the direction of your dreams. Feel free to experiment with different oils as you progress.

Date of Personal AFT Session: _____

[ROUND 1] Step 1 - Set Your Intention/Goal: _____

_____

_____

Rate your intention/goal. How possible does it feel? (Circle One)

Zero Hope - 0 1 2 3 4 5 6 7 8 9 10 - Absolute Confidence

Step 2 - What does the negative voice say that tells you this is not possible? _____

_____

Step 3 - How do you feel when you hear this negative voice (find ONE word)? _____

Step 4 - Where do you feel this emotion in your body? _____

_____

Step 5 - Drift back to an earlier time when you felt the same way - same emotion in the same place in your body. This memory may appear as a single image or a series of memories, like a movie. You might also have nothing come up. Any of these are okay. Notes on previous memory _____ ·

_____

_____

Step 6 - Smell Memory Release Blend (equal parts YL Lavender, YL Frankincense and YL Stress Away) or other oils - specify which oils used: _____

Step 7 - Notice changes to memory, emotion, bodily sensation: _____

_____

_____

Step 8 - Is there a new belief or mindset that has emerged? _____

_____

Step 9 - Read the original intention/goal and rate it again - how possible does it feel now? (circle one)

Zero Hope - 0 1 2 3 4 5 6 7 8 9 10 - Absolute Confidence

(If 8 or higher (or if no negative voice), skip to Step 10 - the Affirmation. If less than 8, return to Step 2 on next page.)

How far have you shifted thus far?

Starting Number: _____ New Number: _____

[ROUND 2] Step 2 - What does the inner voice say that tells you this is not possible? _____

Step 3 - How do you feel when you hear this inner voice (find ONE word)? _____

Step 4 - Where do you feel this emotion in your body? _____

Step 5 - Drift back to an earlier time when you felt the same way - same emotion in the same place in your body. This memory may appear as a single image or a series of memories, like a movie. You might also have nothing come up. Any of these are okay. Notes on previous memory _____

_____
_____

Step 6 - Smell YL Inner Child blend or other oils - specify which oils used:

_____

Step 7 - Notice changes to memory, emotion, bodily sensation: _____

_____
_____

Step 8 - Is there a new belief or mindset that has emerged? _____

_____
_____

Step 9 - Read the original intention/goal and rate it again - how possible does it feel now? (circle one)

Zero Hope - 0 1 2 3 4 5 6 7 8 9 10 - Absolute Confidence

(If 8 or higher (or if no negative voice), skip to Step 10 - the Affirmation. If less than 8, return to Step 2 on next page.)

Look how far you've shifted!

Starting Number: _____ Second Number: _____
Third Number: _____

[ROUND 3] Step 2 - What does the inner voice say that tells you this is not possible? _____

Step 3 - How do you feel when you hear this inner voice (find ONE word)? _____

Step 4 - Where do you feel this emotion in your body? _____

Step 5 - Drift back to an earlier time when you felt the same way - same emotion in the same place in your body. This memory may appear as a single image or a series of memories, like a movie. You might also have nothing come up. Any of these are okay. Notes on previous memory ____

Step 6 - Smell YL Release blend or other oils - specify which oils used: _____

Step 7 - Notice changes to memory, emotion, bodily sensation: _____

Step 8 - Is there a new belief or mindset that has emerged? _____

Step 9 - Read the original intention/goal and rate it again - how possible does it feel now? (circle one)

Zero Hope - 0 1 2 3 4 5 6 7 8 9 10 - Absolute Confidence

Look how far you've shifted!

Starting Number: _____ Second Number: _____
Third Number: _____ Final Number: _____

(Time to set your affirmation, even if you're not yet at an 8 or higher. More shifting will occur during the next 3 steps.)

Step 10 - Affirmation: _____

_____
_____

Step 11 - Stand in Power Pose: Repeat the affirmation for 2 minutes, twice daily, with conviction while standing in a power pose. Smell *Believe™* or *Transformation™* Oil Blend as you do this. (You may choose another transforming oil if you'd like, such as *Build Your Dream™*, *Magnify Your Purpose™*, etc) Chosen Oil & Pose: _____

Repeat for *at least three consecutive days*, or until you create a new affirmation. Check off each box when complete.

Always make sure that your energy feels clear when you say the statement. If you experience inner resistance, use the AFT process to identify and release any negative thoughts, feelings, or memories that come up.

Date	AM	PM

Step 12 - Make Your Plan of Action: _____

_____

_____

_____

_____

_____

Follow-up - What has changed in your life because of THIS Aroma Freedom Technique Session? _____

_____

_____

_____

_____

Program your mind daily! As soon as one affirmation is complete or the goal has been reached, create another. Make affirmations a daily habit and soon you will not feel right unless you have done your daily practice. This will keep you focused in the direction of your dreams. Feel free to experiment with different oils as you progress.

24

Date of Personal AFT Session: _____

[ROUND 1] Step 1 - Set Your Intention/Goal: _____

_____

_____

Rate your intention/goal. How possible does it feel? (Circle One)

Zero Hope - 0 1 2 3 4 5 6 7 8 9 10 - Absolute Confidence

Step 2 - What does the negative voice say that tells you this is not possible? _____

_____

Step 3 - How do you feel when you hear this negative voice (find ONE word)? _____

Step 4 - Where do you feel this emotion in your body? _____

_____

Step 5 - Drift back to an earlier time when you felt the same way - same emotion in the same place in your body. This memory may appear as a single image or a series of memories, like a movie. You might also have nothing come up. Any of these are okay. Notes on previous memory _____

_____

_____

Step 6 - Smell Memory Release Blend (equal parts YL Lavender, YL Frankincense and YL Stress Away) or other oils - specify which oils used: _____

Step 7 - Notice changes to memory, emotion, bodily sensation: _____

_____

_____

Step 8 - Is there a new belief or mindset that has emerged? _____

_____

_____

Step 9 - Read the original intention/goal and rate it again - how possible does it feel now? (circle one)

Zero Hope - 0 1 2 3 4 5 6 7 8 9 10 - Absolute Confidence

(If 8 or higher (or if no negative voice), skip to Step 10 - the Affirmation. If less than 8, return to Step 2 on next page.)

How far have you shifted thus far?

Starting Number: _____ New Number: _____

[ROUND 2] Step 2 - What does the inner voice say that tells you this is not possible? _____

Step 3 - How do you feel when you hear this inner voice (find ONE word)? _____

Step 4 - Where do you feel this emotion in your body? _____

Step 5 - Drift back to an earlier time when you felt the same way - same emotion in the same place in your body. This memory may appear as a single image or a series of memories, like a movie. You might also have nothing come up. Any of these are okay. Notes on previous memory ____

Step 6 - Smell YL Inner Child blend or other oils - specify which oils used:

Step 7 - Notice changes to memory, emotion, bodily sensation: _____

Step 8 - Is there a new belief or mindset that has emerged? _____

Step 9 - Read the original intention/goal and rate it again - how possible does it feel now? (circle one)

Zero Hope - 0 1 2 3 4 5 6 7 8 9 10 - Absolute Confidence

(If 8 or higher (or if no negative voice), skip to Step 10 - the Affirmation. If less than 8, return to Step 2 on next page.)

Look how far you've shifted!

Starting Number: _____ Second Number: _____
Third Number: _____

26

[ROUND 3] Step 2 - What does the inner voice say that tells you this is not possible? _____

Step 3 - How do you feel when you hear this inner voice (find ONE word)? _____

Step 4 - Where do you feel this emotion in your body? _____

Step 5 - Drift back to an earlier time when you felt the same way - same emotion in the same place in your body. This memory may appear as a single image or a series of memories, like a movie. You might also have nothing come up. Any of these are okay. Notes on previous memory _____

_____

Step 6 - Smell YL Release blend or other oils - specify which oils used:

_____

Step 7 - Notice changes to memory, emotion, bodily sensation: _____

_____

Step 8 - Is there a new belief or mindset that has emerged? _____

_____

Step 9 - Read the original intention/goal and rate it again - how possible does it feel now? (circle one)

Zero Hope - 0 1 2 3 4 5 6 7 8 9 10 - Absolute Confidence

Look how far you've shifted!

Starting Number: _____ Second Number: _____
Third Number: _____ Final Number: _____

(Time to set your affirmation, even if you're not yet at an 8 or higher. More shifting will occur during the next 3 steps.)

Step 10 - Affirmation: _____

_____

_____

Step 11 - Stand in Power Pose: Repeat the affirmation for 2 minutes, twice daily, with conviction while standing in a power pose. Smell *Believe™* or *Transformation™* Oil Blend as you do this. (You may choose another transforming oil if you'd like, such as *Build Your Dream™*, *Magnify Your Purpose™*, etc) Chosen Oil & Pose: _____

Repeat for *at least three consecutive days,* or until you create a new affirmation. Check off each box when complete.

Always make sure that your energy feels clear when you say the statement. If you experience inner resistance, use the AFT process to identify and release any negative thoughts, feelings, or memories that come up.

Date	AM	PM

Step 12 - Make Your Plan of Action: _____

_____

_____

_____

_____

_____

Follow-up - What has changed in your life because of THIS Aroma Freedom Technique Session? _____

_____

_____

_____

_____

Program your mind daily! As soon as one affirmation is complete or the goal has been reached, create another. Make affirmations a daily habit and soon you will not feel right unless you have done your daily practice. This will keep you focused in the direction of your dreams. Feel free to experiment with different oils as you progress.

Date of Personal AFT Session: _____

[ROUND 1] Step 1 - Set Your Intention/Goal: _____

_____

Rate your intention/goal. How possible does it feel? (Circle One)

　　Zero Hope - 0 1 2 3 4 5 6 7 8 9 10 - Absolute Confidence

Step 2 - What does the negative voice say that tells you this is not possible? _____

_____
Step 3 - How do you feel when you hear this negative voice (find ONE word)? _____
Step 4 - Where do you feel this emotion in your body? _____

_____
Step 5 - Drift back to an earlier time when you felt the same way - same emotion in the same place in your body. This memory may appear as a single image or a series of memories, like a movie. You might also have nothing come up. Any of these are okay. Notes on previous memory ____

_____

_____
Step 6 - Smell Memory Release Blend (equal parts YL Lavender, YL Frankincense and YL Stress Away) or other oils - specify which oils used: _____
Step 7 - Notice changes to memory, emotion, bodily sensation: _____

_____

_____
Step 8 - Is there a new belief or mindset that has emerged? _____

_____

_____
Step 9 - Read the original intention/goal and rate it again - how possible does it feel now? (circle one)

　　Zero Hope - 0 1 2 3 4 5 6 7 8 9 10 - Absolute Confidence

(If 8 or higher (or if no negative voice), skip to Step 10 - the Affirmation. If less than 8, return to Step 2 on next page.)

How far have you shifted thus far?

Starting Number: _____ New Number: _____

[ROUND 2] Step 2 - What does the inner voice say that tells you this is not possible? _____

Step 3 - How do you feel when you hear this inner voice (find ONE word)? _____
Step 4 - Where do you feel this emotion in your body? _____

Step 5 - Drift back to an earlier time when you felt the same way - same emotion in the same place in your body. This memory may appear as a single image or a series of memories, like a movie. You might also have nothing come up. Any of these are okay. Notes on previous memory _____
_____
_____

Step 6 - Smell YL Inner Child blend or other oils - specify which oils used:
_____

Step 7 - Notice changes to memory, emotion, bodily sensation: _____
_____
_____

Step 8 - Is there a new belief or mindset that has emerged? _____
_____
_____

Step 9 - Read the original intention/goal and rate it again - how possible does it feel now? (circle one)

Zero Hope - 0 1 2 3 4 5 6 7 8 9 10 - Absolute Confidence

(If 8 or higher (or if no negative voice), skip to Step 10 - the Affirmation. If less than 8, return to Step 2 on next page.)

Look how far you've shifted!

Starting Number: _____ Second Number: _____
Third Number: _____

[ROUND 3] Step 2 - What does the inner voice say that tells you this is not possible? _____

Step 3 - How do you feel when you hear this inner voice (find ONE word)? _____

Step 4 - Where do you feel this emotion in your body? _____

Step 5 - Drift back to an earlier time when you felt the same way - same emotion in the same place in your body. This memory may appear as a single image or a series of memories, like a movie. You might also have nothing come up. Any of these are okay. Notes on previous memory _____

Step 6 - Smell YL Release blend or other oils - specify which oils used: _____

Step 7 - Notice changes to memory, emotion, bodily sensation: _____

Step 8 - Is there a new belief or mindset that has emerged? _____

Step 9 - Read the original intention/goal and rate it again - how possible does it feel now? (circle one)

Zero Hope - 0 1 2 3 4 5 6 7 8 9 10 - Absolute Confidence

Look how far you've shifted!

Starting Number: _____ Second Number: _____
Third Number: _____ Final Number: _____

(Time to set your affirmation, even if you're not yet at an 8 or higher. More shifting will occur during the next 3 steps.)

Step 10 - Affirmation: _____

_____
_____

Step 11 - Stand in Power Pose: Repeat the affirmation for 2 minutes, twice daily, with conviction while standing in a power pose. Smell *Believe™* or *Transformation™* Oil Blend as you do this. (You may choose another transforming oil if you'd like, such as *Build Your Dream™, Magnify Your Purpose™*, etc) Chosen Oil & Pose: _____

Repeat for *at least three consecutive days*, or until you create a new affirmation. Check off each box when complete.

Always make sure that your energy feels clear when you say the statement. If you experience inner resistance, use the AFT process to identify and release any negative thoughts, feelings, or memories that come up.

Date	AM	PM

Step 12 - Make Your Plan of Action: _____

_____

_____

_____

_____

_____

Follow-up - What has changed in your life because of THIS Aroma Freedom Technique Session? _____

_____

_____

_____

_____

Program your mind daily! As soon as one affirmation is complete or the goal has been reached, create another. Make affirmations a daily habit and soon you will not feel right unless you have done your daily practice. This will keep you focused in the direction of your dreams. Feel free to experiment with different oils as you progress.

Date of Personal AFT Session: _____

[ROUND 1] Step 1 - Set Your Intention/Goal: _____

_____

_____

Rate your intention/goal. How possible does it feel? (Circle One)

Zero Hope - 0 1 2 3 4 5 6 7 8 9 10 - Absolute Confidence

Step 2 - What does the negative voice say that tells you this is not possible? _____

_____

Step 3 - How do you feel when you hear this negative voice (find ONE word)? _____

Step 4 - Where do you feel this emotion in your body? _____

_____

Step 5 - Drift back to an earlier time when you felt the same way - same emotion in the same place in your body. This memory may appear as a single image or a series of memories, like a movie. You might also have nothing come up. Any of these are okay. Notes on previous memory ____

_____

_____

Step 6 - Smell Memory Release Blend (equal parts YL Lavender, YL Frankincense and YL Stress Away) or other oils - specify which oils used: _____

Step 7 - Notice changes to memory, emotion, bodily sensation: _____

_____

_____

Step 8 - Is there a new belief or mindset that has emerged? _____

_____

_____

Step 9 - Read the original intention/goal and rate it again - how possible does it feel now? (circle one)

Zero Hope - 0 1 2 3 4 5 6 7 8 9 10 - Absolute Confidence

(If 8 or higher (or if no negative voice), skip to Step 10 - the Affirmation. If less than 8, return to Step 2 on next page.)

How far have you shifted thus far?

Starting Number: _____ New Number: _____

[ROUND 2] Step 2 - What does the inner voice say that tells you this is not possible? _____

_____

Step 3 - How do you feel when you hear this inner voice (find ONE word)? _____

Step 4 - Where do you feel this emotion in your body? _____

Step 5 - Drift back to an earlier time when you felt the same way - same emotion in the same place in your body. This memory may appear as a single image or a series of memories, like a movie. You might also have nothing come up. Any of these are okay. Notes on previous memory ____

_____

_____

Step 6 - Smell YL Inner Child blend or other oils - specify which oils used:

_____

Step 7 - Notice changes to memory, emotion, bodily sensation: _____

_____

_____

Step 8 - Is there a new belief or mindset that has emerged? _____

_____

_____

Step 9 - Read the original intention/goal and rate it again - how possible does it feel now? (circle one)

Zero Hope - 0 1 2 3 4 5 6 7 8 9 10 - Absolute Confidence

(If 8 or higher (or if no negative voice), skip to Step 10 - the Affirmation. If less than 8, return to Step 2 on next page.)

Look how far you've shifted!

Starting Number: _____ Second Number: _____
Third Number: _____

34

[ROUND 3] Step 2 - What does the inner voice say that tells you this is not possible? _____

Step 3 - How do you feel when you hear this inner voice (find ONE word)? _____

Step 4 - Where do you feel this emotion in your body? _____

Step 5 - Drift back to an earlier time when you felt the same way - same emotion in the same place in your body. This memory may appear as a single image or a series of memories, like a movie. You might also have nothing come up. Any of these are okay. Notes on previous memory _____

_____

_____

Step 6 - Smell YL Release blend or other oils - specify which oils used:

_____

Step 7 - Notice changes to memory, emotion, bodily sensation: _____

_____

_____

Step 8 - Is there a new belief or mindset that has emerged? _____

_____

_____

Step 9 - Read the original intention/goal and rate it again - how possible does it feel now? (circle one)

Zero Hope - 0 1 2 3 4 5 6 7 8 9 10 - Absolute Confidence

Look how far you've shifted!

Starting Number: _____ Second Number: _____
Third Number: _____ Final Number: _____

(Time to set your affirmation, even if you're not yet at an 8 or higher. More shifting will occur during the next 3 steps.)

Step 10 - Affirmation: _____

_____

_____

Step 11 - Stand in Power Pose: Repeat the affirmation for 2 minutes, twice daily, with conviction while standing in a power pose. Smell *Believe™* or *Transformation™* Oil Blend as you do this. (You may choose another transforming oil if you'd like, such as *Build Your Dream™, Magnify Your Purpose™*, etc) Chosen Oil & Pose: _____

Repeat for *at least three consecutive days*, or until you create a new affirmation. Check off each box when complete.

Always make sure that your energy feels clear when you say the statement. If you experience inner resistance, use the AFT process to identify and release any negative thoughts, feelings, or memories that come up.

Date	AM	PM

Step 12 - Make Your Plan of Action: _____

_____

_____

_____

_____

_____

Follow-up - What has changed in your life because of THIS Aroma Freedom Technique Session? _____

_____

_____

_____

_____

Program your mind daily! As soon as one affirmation is complete or the goal has been reached, create another. Make affirmations a daily habit and soon you will not feel right unless you have done your daily practice. This will keep you focused in the direction of your dreams. Feel free to experiment with different oils as you progress.

Date of Personal AFT Session: _____

[ROUND 1] Step 1 - Set Your Intention/Goal: _____

_____

Rate your intention/goal. How possible does it feel? (Circle One)

Zero Hope - 0 1 2 3 4 5 6 7 8 9 10 - Absolute Confidence

Step 2 - What does the negative voice say that tells you this is not possible? _____

Step 3 - How do you feel when you hear this negative voice (find ONE word)? _____

Step 4 - Where do you feel this emotion in your body? _____

_____

Step 5 - Drift back to an earlier time when you felt the same way - same emotion in the same place in your body. This memory may appear as a single image or a series of memories, like a movie. You might also have nothing come up. Any of these are okay. Notes on previous memory ____

_____

Step 6 - Smell Memory Release Blend (equal parts YL Lavender, YL Frankincense and YL Stress Away) or other oils - specify which oils used: _____

Step 7 - Notice changes to memory, emotion, bodily sensation: _____

_____

Step 8 - Is there a new belief or mindset that has emerged? _____

_____

Step 9 - Read the original intention/goal and rate it again - how possible does it feel now? (circle one)

Zero Hope - 0 1 2 3 4 5 6 7 8 9 10 - Absolute Confidence

(If 8 or higher (or if no negative voice), skip to Step 10 - the Affirmation. If less than 8, return to Step 2 on next page.)

How far have you shifted thus far?

Starting Number: _____ New Number: _____

[ROUND 2] Step 2 - What does the inner voice say that tells you this is not possible? _____

_____

Step 3 - How do you feel when you hear this inner voice (find ONE word)? _____

Step 4 - Where do you feel this emotion in your body? _____

_____

Step 5 - Drift back to an earlier time when you felt the same way - same emotion in the same place in your body. This memory may appear as a single image or a series of memories, like a movie. You might also have nothing come up. Any of these are okay. Notes on previous memory _____

_____

_____

Step 6 - Smell YL Inner Child blend or other oils - specify which oils used:

_____

Step 7 - Notice changes to memory, emotion, bodily sensation: _____

_____

_____

Step 8 - Is there a new belief or mindset that has emerged? _____

_____

_____

Step 9 - Read the original intention/goal and rate it again - how possible does it feel now? (circle one)

Zero Hope - 0 1 2 3 4 5 6 7 8 9 10 - Absolute Confidence

(If 8 or higher (or if no negative voice), skip to Step 10 - the Affirmation. If less than 8, return to Step 2 on next page.)

Look how far you've shifted!

Starting Number: _____ Second Number: _____

Third Number: _____

[ROUND 3] Step 2 - What does the inner voice say that tells you this is not possible? _____

Step 3 - How do you feel when you hear this inner voice (find ONE word)? _____

Step 4 - Where do you feel this emotion in your body? _____

Step 5 - Drift back to an earlier time when you felt the same way - same emotion in the same place in your body. This memory may appear as a single image or a series of memories, like a movie. You might also have nothing come up. Any of these are okay. Notes on previous memory _____
_____

Step 6 - Smell YL Release blend or other oils - specify which oils used:
_____

Step 7 - Notice changes to memory, emotion, bodily sensation: _____
_____

Step 8 - Is there a new belief or mindset that has emerged? _____
_____

Step 9 - Read the original intention/goal and rate it again - how possible does it feel now? (circle one)

Zero Hope - 0 1 2 3 4 5 6 7 8 9 10 - Absolute Confidence

Look how far you've shifted!

Starting Number: _____ Second Number: _____
Third Number: _____ Final Number: _____

(Time to set your affirmation, even if you're not yet at an 8 or higher. More shifting will occur during the next 3 steps.)

Step 10 - Affirmation: _____
_____
_____

Step 11 - Stand in Power Pose: Repeat the affirmation for 2 minutes, twice daily, with conviction while standing in a power pose. Smell *Believe*™ or *Transformation*™ Oil Blend as you do this. (You may choose another transforming oil if you'd like, such as *Build Your Dream*™, *Magnify Your Purpose*™, etc) Chosen Oil & Pose: _____

Repeat for *at least three consecutive days*, or until you create a new affirmation. Check off each box when complete.

Always make sure that your energy feels clear when you say the statement. If you experience inner resistance, use the AFT process to identify and release any negative thoughts, feelings, or memories that come up.

Date	AM	PM

Step 12 - Make Your Plan of Action: _____

_____

_____

_____

_____

_____

Follow-up - What has changed in your life because of THIS Aroma Freedom Technique Session? _____

_____

_____

_____

_____

Program your mind daily! As soon as one affirmation is complete or the goal has been reached, create another. Make affirmations a daily habit and soon you will not feel right unless you have done your daily practice. This will keep you focused in the direction of your dreams. Feel free to experiment with different oils as you progress.

Date of Personal AFT Session: _____

[ROUND 1] Step 1 - Set Your Intention/Goal: _____

_____

Rate your intention/goal. How possible does it feel? (Circle One)

Zero Hope - 0 1 2 3 4 5 6 7 8 9 10 - Absolute Confidence

Step 2 - What does the negative voice say that tells you this is not possible? _____

Step 3 - How do you feel when you hear this negative voice (find ONE word)? _____

Step 4 - Where do you feel this emotion in your body? _____

_____

Step 5 - Drift back to an earlier time when you felt the same way - same emotion in the same place in your body. This memory may appear as a single image or a series of memories, like a movie. You might also have nothing come up. Any of these are okay. Notes on previous memory _____

_____

Step 6 - Smell Memory Release Blend (equal parts YL Lavender, YL Frankincense and YL Stress Away) or other oils - specify which oils used: _____

Step 7 - Notice changes to memory, emotion, bodily sensation: _____

_____

Step 8 - Is there a new belief or mindset that has emerged? _____

_____

Step 9 - Read the original intention/goal and rate it again - how possible does it feel now? (circle one)

Zero Hope - 0 1 2 3 4 5 6 7 8 9 10 - Absolute Confidence

(If 8 or higher (or if no negative voice), skip to Step 10 - the Affirmation. If less than 8, return to Step 2 on next page.)

How far have you shifted thus far?

Starting Number: _____ New Number: _____

[ROUND 2] Step 2 - What does the inner voice say that tells you this is not possible? _____

_____

Step 3 - How do you feel when you hear this inner voice (find ONE word)? _____
Step 4 - Where do you feel this emotion in your body? _____

_____

Step 5 - Drift back to an earlier time when you felt the same way - same emotion in the same place in your body. This memory may appear as a single image or a series of memories, like a movie. You might also have nothing come up. Any of these are okay. Notes on previous memory _____

_____

_____

Step 6 - Smell YL Inner Child blend or other oils - specify which oils used:

_____

Step 7 - Notice changes to memory, emotion, bodily sensation: _____

_____

_____

Step 8 - Is there a new belief or mindset that has emerged? _____

_____

_____

Step 9 - Read the original intention/goal and rate it again - how possible does it feel now? (circle one)

Zero Hope - 0 1 2 3 4 5 6 7 8 9 10 - Absolute Confidence

(If 8 or higher (or if no negative voice), skip to Step 10 - the Affirmation. If less than 8, return to Step 2 on next page.)

Look how far you've shifted!

Starting Number: _____ Second Number: _____
Third Number: _____

[ROUND 3] Step 2 - What does the inner voice say that tells you this is not possible? _____

Step 3 - How do you feel when you hear this inner voice (find ONE word)? _____

Step 4 - Where do you feel this emotion in your body? _____

Step 5 - Drift back to an earlier time when you felt the same way - same emotion in the same place in your body. This memory may appear as a single image or a series of memories, like a movie. You might also have nothing come up. Any of these are okay. Notes on previous memory _____

_____

Step 6 - Smell YL Release blend or other oils - specify which oils used:

_____

Step 7 - Notice changes to memory, emotion, bodily sensation: _____

_____

Step 8 - Is there a new belief or mindset that has emerged? _____

_____

Step 9 - Read the original intention/goal and rate it again - how possible does it feel now? (circle one)

Zero Hope - 0 1 2 3 4 5 6 7 8 9 10 - Absolute Confidence

Look how far you've shifted!

Starting Number: _____ Second Number: _____
Third Number: _____ Final Number: _____

(Time to set your affirmation, even if you're not yet at an 8 or higher. More shifting will occur during the next 3 steps.)

Step 10 - Affirmation: _____

_____

_____

Step 11 - Stand in Power Pose: Repeat the affirmation for 2 minutes, twice daily, with conviction while standing in a power pose. Smell *Believe™* or *Transformation™* Oil Blend as you do this. (You may choose another transforming oil if you'd like, such as *Build Your Dream™, Magnify Your Purpose™*, etc) Chosen Oil & Pose: _____

Repeat for *at least three consecutive days,* or until you create a new affirmation. Check off each box when complete.

Always make sure that your energy feels clear when you say the statement. If you experience inner resistance, use the AFT process to identify and release any negative thoughts, feelings, or memories that come up.

Date	AM	PM

Step 12 - Make Your Plan of Action: _____

_____

_____

_____

_____

_____

Follow-up - What has changed in your life because of THIS Aroma Freedom Technique Session? _____

_____

_____

_____

_____

Program your mind daily! As soon as one affirmation is complete or the goal has been reached, create another. Make affirmations a daily habit and soon you will not feel right unless you have done your daily practice. This will keep you focused in the direction of your dreams. Feel free to experiment with different oils as you progress.

Date of Personal AFT Session: _____

[ROUND 1] Step 1 - Set Your Intention/Goal: _____

_____

Rate your intention/goal. How possible does it feel? (Circle One)

Zero Hope - 0 1 2 3 4 5 6 7 8 9 10 - Absolute Confidence

Step 2 - What does the negative voice say that tells you this is not possible? _____

Step 3 - How do you feel when you hear this negative voice (find ONE word)? _____

Step 4 - Where do you feel this emotion in your body? _____

Step 5 - Drift back to an earlier time when you felt the same way - same emotion in the same place in your body. This memory may appear as a single image or a series of memories, like a movie. You might also have nothing come up. Any of these are okay. Notes on previous memory _____

_____

Step 6 - Smell Memory Release Blend (equal parts YL Lavender, YL Frankincense and YL Stress Away) or other oils - specify which oils used: _____

Step 7 - Notice changes to memory, emotion, bodily sensation: _____

_____

Step 8 - Is there a new belief or mindset that has emerged? _____

_____

Step 9 - Read the original intention/goal and rate it again - how possible does it feel now? (circle one)

Zero Hope - 0 1 2 3 4 5 6 7 8 9 10 - Absolute Confidence

(If 8 or higher (or if no negative voice), skip to Step 10 - the Affirmation. If less than 8, return to Step 2 on next page.)

How far have you shifted thus far?

Starting Number: _____ New Number: _____

[ROUND 2] Step 2 - What does the inner voice say that tells you this is not possible? _____

Step 3 - How do you feel when you hear this inner voice (find ONE word)? _____
Step 4 - Where do you feel this emotion in your body? _____

Step 5 - Drift back to an earlier time when you felt the same way - same emotion in the same place in your body. This memory may appear as a single image or a series of memories, like a movie. You might also have nothing come up. Any of these are okay. Notes on previous memory _____
_____
_____

Step 6 - Smell YL Inner Child blend or other oils - specify which oils used:
_____

Step 7 - Notice changes to memory, emotion, bodily sensation: _____
_____
_____

Step 8 - Is there a new belief or mindset that has emerged? _____
_____
_____

Step 9 - Read the original intention/goal and rate it again - how possible does it feel now? (circle one)

Zero Hope - 0 1 2 3 4 5 6 7 8 9 10 - Absolute Confidence

(If 8 or higher (or if no negative voice), skip to Step 10 - the Affirmation. If less than 8, return to Step 2 on next page.)

Look how far you've shifted!

Starting Number: _____ Second Number: _____
Third Number: _____

[ROUND 3] Step 2 - What does the inner voice say that tells you this is not possible? _____

Step 3 - How do you feel when you hear this inner voice (find ONE word)? _____
Step 4 - Where do you feel this emotion in your body? _____

Step 5 - Drift back to an earlier time when you felt the same way - same emotion in the same place in your body. This memory may appear as a single image or a series of memories, like a movie. You might also have nothing come up. Any of these are okay. Notes on previous memory _____

Step 6 - Smell YL Release blend or other oils - specify which oils used: _____

Step 7 - Notice changes to memory, emotion, bodily sensation: _____

Step 8 - Is there a new belief or mindset that has emerged? _____

Step 9 - Read the original intention/goal and rate it again - how possible does it feel now? (circle one)

Zero Hope - 0 1 2 3 4 5 6 7 8 9 10 - Absolute Confidence

Look how far you've shifted!

Starting Number: _____ Second Number: _____
Third Number: _____ Final Number: _____

(Time to set your affirmation, even if you're not yet at an 8 or higher. More shifting will occur during the next 3 steps.)

Step 10 - Affirmation: _____

47

Step 11 - Stand in Power Pose: Repeat the affirmation for 2 minutes, twice daily, with conviction while standing in a power pose. Smell *Believe™* or *Transformation™* Oil Blend as you do this. (You may choose another transforming oil if you'd like, such as *Build Your Dream™*, *Magnify Your Purpose™*, etc) Chosen Oil & Pose: _____

Repeat for *at least three consecutive days*, or until you create a new affirmation. Check off each box when complete.

Always make sure that your energy feels clear when you say the statement. If you experience inner resistance, use the AFT process to identify and release any negative thoughts, feelings, or memories that come up.

Date	AM	PM

Step 12 - Make Your Plan of Action: _____

_____

_____

_____

_____

_____

Follow-up - What has changed in your life because of THIS Aroma Freedom Technique Session? _____

_____

_____

_____

_____

Program your mind daily! As soon as one affirmation is complete or the goal has been reached, create another. Make affirmations a daily habit and soon you will not feel right unless you have done your daily practice. This will keep you focused in the direction of your dreams. Feel free to experiment with different oils as you progress.

Date of Personal AFT Session: _____

[ROUND 1] Step 1 - Set Your Intention/Goal: _____

_____

_____

Rate your intention/goal. How possible does it feel? (Circle One)

Zero Hope - 0 1 2 3 4 5 6 7 8 9 10 - Absolute Confidence

Step 2 - What does the negative voice say that tells you this is not possible? _____

_____

Step 3 - How do you feel when you hear this negative voice (find ONE word)? _____

Step 4 - Where do you feel this emotion in your body? _____

_____

Step 5 - Drift back to an earlier time when you felt the same way - same emotion in the same place in your body. This memory may appear as a single image or a series of memories, like a movie. You might also have nothing come up. Any of these are okay. Notes on previous memory _____

_____

_____

Step 6 - Smell Memory Release Blend (equal parts YL Lavender, YL Frankincense and YL Stress Away) or other oils - specify which oils used: _____

Step 7 - Notice changes to memory, emotion, bodily sensation: _____

_____

_____

Step 8 - Is there a new belief or mindset that has emerged? _____

_____

_____

Step 9 - Read the original intention/goal and rate it again - how possible does it feel now? (circle one)

Zero Hope - 0 1 2 3 4 5 6 7 8 9 10 - Absolute Confidence

(If 8 or higher (or if no negative voice), skip to Step 10 - the Affirmation. If less than 8, return to Step 2 on next page.)

How far have you shifted thus far?

Starting Number: _____ New Number: _____

[ROUND 2] Step 2 - What does the inner voice say that tells you this is not possible? _____

Step 3 - How do you feel when you hear this inner voice (find ONE word)? _____
Step 4 - Where do you feel this emotion in your body? _____

Step 5 - Drift back to an earlier time when you felt the same way - same emotion in the same place in your body. This memory may appear as a single image or a series of memories, like a movie. You might also have nothing come up. Any of these are okay. Notes on previous memory _____

_____

Step 6 - Smell YL Inner Child blend or other oils - specify which oils used:

_____

Step 7 - Notice changes to memory, emotion, bodily sensation: _____

_____

Step 8 - Is there a new belief or mindset that has emerged? _____

_____

Step 9 - Read the original intention/goal and rate it again - how possible does it feel now? (circle one)

Zero Hope - 0 1 2 3 4 5 6 7 8 9 10 - Absolute Confidence

(If 8 or higher (or if no negative voice), skip to Step 10 - the Affirmation. If less than 8, return to Step 2 on next page.)

Look how far you've shifted!

Starting Number: _____ Second Number: _____
Third Number: _____

[ROUND 3] Step 2 - What does the inner voice say that tells you this is not possible? _____

Step 3 - How do you feel when you hear this inner voice (find ONE word)? _____

Step 4 - Where do you feel this emotion in your body? _____

Step 5 - Drift back to an earlier time when you felt the same way - same emotion in the same place in your body. This memory may appear as a single image or a series of memories, like a movie. You might also have nothing come up. Any of these are okay. Notes on previous memory _____

_____

Step 6 - Smell YL Release blend or other oils - specify which oils used:

_____

Step 7 - Notice changes to memory, emotion, bodily sensation: _____

_____

Step 8 - Is there a new belief or mindset that has emerged? _____

_____

Step 9 - Read the original intention/goal and rate it again - how possible does it feel now? (circle one)

Zero Hope - 0 1 2 3 4 5 6 7 8 9 10 - Absolute Confidence

Look how far you've shifted!

Starting Number: _____ Second Number: _____
Third Number: _____ Final Number: _____

(Time to set your affirmation, even if you're not yet at an 8 or higher. More shifting will occur during the next 3 steps.)

Step 10 - Affirmation: _____

_____

_____

Step 11 - Stand in Power Pose: Repeat the affirmation for 2 minutes, twice daily, with conviction while standing in a power pose. Smell *Believe™* or *Transformation™* Oil Blend as you do this. (You may choose another transforming oil if you'd like, such as *Build Your Dream™*, *Magnify Your Purpose™*, etc) Chosen Oil & Pose: _____

Repeat for *at least three consecutive days*, or until you create a new affirmation. Check off each box when complete.

Always make sure that your energy feels clear when you say the statement. If you experience inner resistance, use the AFT process to identify and release any negative thoughts, feelings, or memories that come up.

Date	AM	PM

Step 12 - Make Your Plan of Action: _____

_____

_____

_____

_____

_____

Follow-up - What has changed in your life because of THIS Aroma Freedom Technique Session? _____

_____

_____

_____

_____

Program your mind daily! As soon as one affirmation is complete or the goal has been reached, create another. Make affirmations a daily habit and soon you will not feel right unless you have done your daily practice. This will keep you focused in the direction of your dreams. Feel free to experiment with different oils as you progress.

Date of Personal AFT Session: _____

[ROUND 1] Step 1 - Set Your Intention/Goal: _____

_____

Rate your intention/goal. How possible does it feel? (Circle One)

Zero Hope - 0 1 2 3 4 5 6 7 8 9 10 - Absolute Confidence

Step 2 - What does the negative voice say that tells you this is not possible? _____

Step 3 - How do you feel when you hear this negative voice (find ONE word)? _____

Step 4 - Where do you feel this emotion in your body? _____

_____

Step 5 - Drift back to an earlier time when you felt the same way - same emotion in the same place in your body. This memory may appear as a single image or a series of memories, like a movie. You might also have nothing come up. Any of these are okay. Notes on previous memory ____

_____

Step 6 - Smell Memory Release Blend (equal parts YL Lavender, YL Frankincense and YL Stress Away) or other oils - specify which oils used: _____

Step 7 - Notice changes to memory, emotion, bodily sensation: _____

_____

Step 8 - Is there a new belief or mindset that has emerged? _____

_____

Step 9 - Read the original intention/goal and rate it again - how possible does it feel now? (circle one)

Zero Hope - 0 1 2 3 4 5 6 7 8 9 10 - Absolute Confidence

(If 8 or higher (or if no negative voice), skip to Step 10 - the Affirmation. If less than 8, return to Step 2 on next page.)

How far have you shifted thus far?

Starting Number: _____ New Number: _____

[ROUND 2] Step 2 - What does the inner voice say that tells you this is not possible? _____

_____

Step 3 - How do you feel when you hear this inner voice (find ONE word)? _____

Step 4 - Where do you feel this emotion in your body? _____

_____

Step 5 - Drift back to an earlier time when you felt the same way - same emotion in the same place in your body. This memory may appear as a single image or a series of memories, like a movie. You might also have nothing come up. Any of these are okay. Notes on previous memory _____

_____

_____

Step 6 - Smell YL Inner Child blend or other oils - specify which oils used:

_____

Step 7 - Notice changes to memory, emotion, bodily sensation: _____

_____

_____

Step 8 - Is there a new belief or mindset that has emerged? _____

_____

Step 9 - Read the original intention/goal and rate it again - how possible does it feel now? (circle one)

Zero Hope - 0 1 2 3 4 5 6 7 8 9 10 - Absolute Confidence

(If 8 or higher (or if no negative voice), skip to Step 10 - the Affirmation. If less than 8, return to Step 2 on next page.)

Look how far you've shifted!

Starting Number: _____ Second Number: _____
Third Number: _____

[ROUND 3] Step 2 - What does the inner voice say that tells you this is not possible? _____

_____

Step 3 - How do you feel when you hear this inner voice (find ONE word)? _____

Step 4 - Where do you feel this emotion in your body? _____

_____

Step 5 - Drift back to an earlier time when you felt the same way - same emotion in the same place in your body. This memory may appear as a single image or a series of memories, like a movie. You might also have nothing come up. Any of these are okay. Notes on previous memory _____

_____

Step 6 - Smell YL Release blend or other oils - specify which oils used:

_____

Step 7 - Notice changes to memory, emotion, bodily sensation: _____

_____

Step 8 - Is there a new belief or mindset that has emerged? _____

_____

Step 9 - Read the original intention/goal and rate it again - how possible does it feel now? (circle one)

Zero Hope - 0 1 2 3 4 5 6 7 8 9 10 - Absolute Confidence

Look how far you've shifted!

Starting Number: _____ Second Number: _____
Third Number: _____ Final Number: _____

(Time to set your affirmation, even if you're not yet at an 8 or higher. More shifting will occur during the next 3 steps.)

Step 10 - Affirmation: _____

_____

_____

Step 11 - Stand in Power Pose: Repeat the affirmation for 2 minutes, twice daily, with conviction while standing in a power pose. Smell *Believe*™ or *Transformation*™ Oil Blend as you do this. (You may choose another transforming oil if you'd like, such as *Build Your Dream*™, *Magnify Your Purpose*™, etc) Chosen Oil & Pose: _____

Repeat for *at least three consecutive days*, or until you create a new affirmation. Check off each box when complete.

Always make sure that your energy feels clear when you say the statement. If you experience inner resistance, use the AFT process to identify and release any negative thoughts, feelings, or memories that come up.

Date	AM	PM

Step 12 - Make Your Plan of Action: _____

_____

_____

_____

_____

_____

Follow-up - What has changed in your life because of THIS Aroma Freedom Technique Session? _____

_____

_____

_____

_____

Program your mind daily! As soon as one affirmation is complete or the goal has been reached, create another. Make affirmations a daily habit and soon you will not feel right unless you have done your daily practice. This will keep you focused in the direction of your dreams. Feel free to experiment with different oils as you progress.

Date of Personal AFT Session: _____

[ROUND 1] Step 1 - Set Your Intention/Goal: _____

_____

Rate your intention/goal. How possible does it feel? (Circle One)

   Zero Hope - 0 1 2 3 4 5 6 7 8 9 10 - Absolute Confidence

Step 2 - What does the negative voice say that tells you this is not possible? _____

Step 3 - How do you feel when you hear this negative voice (find ONE word)? _____

Step 4 - Where do you feel this emotion in your body? _____

Step 5 - Drift back to an earlier time when you felt the same way - same emotion in the same place in your body. This memory may appear as a single image or a series of memories, like a movie. You might also have nothing come up. Any of these are okay. Notes on previous memory _____

_____

Step 6 - Smell Memory Release Blend (equal parts YL Lavender, YL Frankincense and YL Stress Away) or other oils - specify which oils used: _____

Step 7 - Notice changes to memory, emotion, bodily sensation: _____

_____

Step 8 - Is there a new belief or mindset that has emerged? _____

_____

Step 9 - Read the original intention/goal and rate it again - how possible does it feel now? (circle one)

   Zero Hope - 0 1 2 3 4 5 6 7 8 9 10 - Absolute Confidence

(If 8 or higher (or if no negative voice), skip to Step 10 - the Affirmation. If less than 8, return to Step 2 on next page.)

How far have you shifted thus far?

Starting Number: _____ New Number: _____

[ROUND 2] Step 2 - What does the inner voice say that tells you this is not possible? _____

Step 3 - How do you feel when you hear this inner voice (find ONE word)? _____
Step 4 - Where do you feel this emotion in your body? _____

Step 5 - Drift back to an earlier time when you felt the same way - same emotion in the same place in your body. This memory may appear as a single image or a series of memories, like a movie. You might also have nothing come up. Any of these are okay. Notes on previous memory _____
_____
_____

Step 6 - Smell YL Inner Child blend or other oils - specify which oils used:
_____

Step 7 - Notice changes to memory, emotion, bodily sensation: _____
_____
_____

Step 8 - Is there a new belief or mindset that has emerged? _____
_____
_____

Step 9 - Read the original intention/goal and rate it again - how possible does it feel now? (circle one)

Zero Hope - 0 1 2 3 4 5 6 7 8 9 10 - Absolute Confidence

(If 8 or higher (or if no negative voice), skip to Step 10 - the Affirmation. If less than 8, return to Step 2 on next page.)

Look how far you've shifted!

Starting Number: _____ Second Number: _____
Third Number: _____

[ROUND 3] Step 2 - What does the inner voice say that tells you this is not possible? _____

_____

Step 3 - How do you feel when you hear this inner voice (find ONE word)? _____

Step 4 - Where do you feel this emotion in your body? _____

_____

Step 5 - Drift back to an earlier time when you felt the same way - same emotion in the same place in your body. This memory may appear as a single image or a series of memories, like a movie. You might also have nothing come up. Any of these are okay. Notes on previous memory _____

_____

Step 6 - Smell YL Release blend or other oils - specify which oils used:

_____

Step 7 - Notice changes to memory, emotion, bodily sensation: _____

_____

Step 8 - Is there a new belief or mindset that has emerged? _____

_____

Step 9 - Read the original intention/goal and rate it again - how possible does it feel now? (circle one)

Zero Hope - 0 1 2 3 4 5 6 7 8 9 10 - Absolute Confidence

Look how far you've shifted!

Starting Number: _____ Second Number: _____
Third Number: _____ Final Number: _____

(Time to set your affirmation, even if you're not yet at an 8 or higher. More shifting will occur during the next 3 steps.)

Step 10 - Affirmation: _____

_____

_____

Step 11 - Stand in Power Pose: Repeat the affirmation for 2 minutes, twice daily, with conviction while standing in a power pose. Smell *Believe*™ or *Transformation*™ Oil Blend as you do this. (You may choose another transforming oil if you'd like, such as *Build Your Dream*™, *Magnify Your Purpose*™, etc) Chosen Oil & Pose: _____

Repeat for *at least three consecutive days*, or until you create a new affirmation. Check off each box when complete.

Always make sure that your energy feels clear when you say the statement. If you experience inner resistance, use the AFT process to identify and release any negative thoughts, feelings, or memories that come up.

Date	AM	PM

Step 12 - Make Your Plan of Action: _____

_____

_____

_____

_____

_____

Follow-up - What has changed in your life because of THIS Aroma Freedom Technique Session? _____

_____

_____

_____

_____

Program your mind daily! As soon as one affirmation is complete or the goal has been reached, create another. Make affirmations a daily habit and soon you will not feel right unless you have done your daily practice. This will keep you focused in the direction of your dreams. Feel free to experiment with different oils as you progress.

Date of Personal AFT Session: _____

[ROUND 1] Step 1 - Set Your Intention/Goal: _____
_____

Rate your intention/goal. How possible does it feel? (Circle One)

    Zero Hope - 0 1 2 3 4 5 6 7 8 9 10 - Absolute Confidence

Step 2 - What does the negative voice say that tells you this is not possible? _____
_____

Step 3 - How do you feel when you hear this negative voice (find ONE word)? _____

Step 4 - Where do you feel this emotion in your body? _____
_____

Step 5 - Drift back to an earlier time when you felt the same way - same emotion in the same place in your body. This memory may appear as a single image or a series of memories, like a movie. You might also have nothing come up. Any of these are okay. Notes on previous memory ____
_____

Step 6 - Smell Memory Release Blend (equal parts YL Lavender, YL Frankincense and YL Stress Away) or other oils - specify which oils used: _____

Step 7 - Notice changes to memory, emotion, bodily sensation: _____
_____

Step 8 - Is there a new belief or mindset that has emerged? _____
_____

Step 9 - Read the original intention/goal and rate it again - how possible does it feel now? (circle one)

    Zero Hope - 0 1 2 3 4 5 6 7 8 9 10 - Absolute Confidence

(If 8 or higher (or if no negative voice), skip to Step 10 - the Affirmation. If less than 8, return to Step 2 on next page.)

How far have you shifted thus far?

Starting Number: _____ New Number: _____

[ROUND 2] Step 2 - What does the inner voice say that tells you this is not possible? _____

_____

Step 3 - How do you feel when you hear this inner voice (find ONE word)? _____

Step 4 - Where do you feel this emotion in your body? _____

_____

Step 5 - Drift back to an earlier time when you felt the same way - same emotion in the same place in your body. This memory may appear as a single image or a series of memories, like a movie. You might also have nothing come up. Any of these are okay. Notes on previous memory _____

_____

_____

Step 6 - Smell YL Inner Child blend or other oils - specify which oils used:

_____

Step 7 - Notice changes to memory, emotion, bodily sensation: _____

_____

_____

Step 8 - Is there a new belief or mindset that has emerged? _____

_____

_____

Step 9 - Read the original intention/goal and rate it again - how possible does it feel now? (circle one)

Zero Hope - 0 1 2 3 4 5 6 7 8 9 10 - Absolute Confidence

(If 8 or higher (or if no negative voice), skip to Step 10 - the Affirmation. If less than 8, return to Step 2 on next page.)

Look how far you've shifted!

Starting Number: _____ Second Number: _____
Third Number: _____

[ROUND 3] Step 2 - What does the inner voice say that tells you this is not possible? _____

_____

Step 3 - How do you feel when you hear this inner voice (find ONE word)? _____

Step 4 - Where do you feel this emotion in your body? _____

_____

Step 5 - Drift back to an earlier time when you felt the same way - same emotion in the same place in your body. This memory may appear as a single image or a series of memories, like a movie. You might also have nothing come up. Any of these are okay. Notes on previous memory _____

_____

_____

Step 6 - Smell YL Release blend or other oils - specify which oils used:

_____

Step 7 - Notice changes to memory, emotion, bodily sensation: _____

_____

_____

Step 8 - Is there a new belief or mindset that has emerged? _____

_____

_____

Step 9 - Read the original intention/goal and rate it again - how possible does it feel now? (circle one)

Zero Hope - 0 1 2 3 4 5 6 7 8 9 10 - Absolute Confidence

Look how far you've shifted!

Starting Number: _____ Second Number: _____
Third Number: _____ Final Number: _____

(Time to set your affirmation, even if you're not yet at an 8 or higher. More shifting will occur during the next 3 steps.)

Step 10 - Affirmation: _____

_____

_____

Step 11 - Stand in Power Pose: Repeat the affirmation for 2 minutes, twice daily, with conviction while standing in a power pose. Smell *Believe*™ or *Transformation*™ Oil Blend as you do this. (You may choose another transforming oil if you'd like, such as *Build Your Dream*™, *Magnify Your Purpose*™, etc) Chosen Oil & Pose: _____

Repeat for *at least three consecutive days*, or until you create a new affirmation. Check off each box when complete.

Always make sure that your energy feels clear when you say the statement. If you experience inner resistance, use the AFT process to identify and release any negative thoughts, feelings, or memories that come up.

Date	AM	PM

Step 12 - Make Your Plan of Action: _____

_____

_____

_____

_____

_____

Follow-up - What has changed in your life because of THIS Aroma Freedom Technique Session? _____

_____

_____

_____

_____

Program your mind daily! As soon as one affirmation is complete or the goal has been reached, create another. Make affirmations a daily habit and soon you will not feel right unless you have done your daily practice. This will keep you focused in the direction of your dreams. Feel free to experiment with different oils as you progress.

Date of Personal AFT Session: _____

[ROUND 1] Step 1 - Set Your Intention/Goal: _____
_____
_____

Rate your intention/goal. How possible does it feel? (Circle One)

Zero Hope - 0 1 2 3 4 5 6 7 8 9 10 - Absolute Confidence

Step 2 - What does the negative voice say that tells you this is not possible? _____
_____

Step 3 - How do you feel when you hear this negative voice (find ONE word)? _____

Step 4 - Where do you feel this emotion in your body? _____
_____

Step 5 - Drift back to an earlier time when you felt the same way - same emotion in the same place in your body. This memory may appear as a single image or a series of memories, like a movie. You might also have nothing come up. Any of these are okay. Notes on previous memory _____
_____
_____

Step 6 - Smell Memory Release Blend (equal parts YL Lavender, YL Frankincense and YL Stress Away) or other oils - specify which oils used: _____

Step 7 - Notice changes to memory, emotion, bodily sensation: _____
_____
_____

Step 8 - Is there a new belief or mindset that has emerged? _____
_____
_____

Step 9 - Read the original intention/goal and rate it again - how possible does it feel now? (circle one)

Zero Hope - 0 1 2 3 4 5 6 7 8 9 10 - Absolute Confidence

(If 8 or higher (or if no negative voice), skip to Step 10 - the Affirmation. If less than 8, return to Step 2 on next page.)

65

How far have you shifted thus far?

Starting Number: _____ New Number: _____

[ROUND 2] Step 2 - What does the inner voice say that tells you this is not possible? _____

_____

Step 3 - How do you feel when you hear this inner voice (find ONE word)? _____

Step 4 - Where do you feel this emotion in your body? _____

_____

Step 5 - Drift back to an earlier time when you felt the same way - same emotion in the same place in your body. This memory may appear as a single image or a series of memories, like a movie. You might also have nothing come up. Any of these are okay. Notes on previous memory _____

_____

_____

Step 6 - Smell YL Inner Child blend or other oils - specify which oils used:

_____

Step 7 - Notice changes to memory, emotion, bodily sensation: _____

_____

_____

Step 8 - Is there a new belief or mindset that has emerged? _____

_____

_____

Step 9 - Read the original intention/goal and rate it again - how possible does it feel now? (circle one)

Zero Hope - 0 1 2 3 4 5 6 7 8 9 10 - Absolute Confidence

(If 8 or higher (or if no negative voice), skip to Step 10 - the Affirmation. If less than 8, return to Step 2 on next page.)

Look how far you've shifted!

Starting Number: _____ Second Number: _____

Third Number: _____

[ROUND 3] Step 2 - What does the inner voice say that tells you this is not possible? _____

Step 3 - How do you feel when you hear this inner voice (find ONE word)? _____

Step 4 - Where do you feel this emotion in your body? _____

Step 5 - Drift back to an earlier time when you felt the same way - same emotion in the same place in your body. This memory may appear as a single image or a series of memories, like a movie. You might also have nothing come up. Any of these are okay. Notes on previous memory _____

_____

Step 6 - Smell YL Release blend or other oils - specify which oils used:

_____

Step 7 - Notice changes to memory, emotion, bodily sensation: _____

_____

Step 8 - Is there a new belief or mindset that has emerged? _____

_____

Step 9 - Read the original intention/goal and rate it again - how possible does it feel now? (circle one)

Zero Hope - 0 1 2 3 4 5 6 7 8 9 10 - Absolute Confidence

Look how far you've shifted!

Starting Number: _____ Second Number: _____
Third Number: _____ Final Number: _____

(Time to set your affirmation, even if you're not yet at an 8 or higher. More shifting will occur during the next 3 steps.)

Step 10 - Affirmation: _____

_____

_____

Step 11 - Stand in Power Pose: Repeat the affirmation for 2 minutes, twice daily, with conviction while standing in a power pose. Smell *Believe*™ or *Transformation*™ Oil Blend as you do this. (You may choose another transforming oil if you'd like, such as *Build Your Dream*™, *Magnify Your Purpose*™, etc) Chosen Oil & Pose: _____

Repeat for *at least three consecutive days*, or until you create a new affirmation. Check off each box when complete.

Always make sure that your energy feels clear when you say the statement. If you experience inner resistance, use the AFT process to identify and release any negative thoughts, feelings, or memories that come up.

Date	AM	PM

Step 12 - Make Your Plan of Action: _____

_____

_____

_____

_____

_____

Follow-up - What has changed in your life because of THIS Aroma Freedom Technique Session? _____

_____

_____

_____

_____

Program your mind daily! As soon as one affirmation is complete or the goal has been reached, create another. Make affirmations a daily habit and soon you will not feel right unless you have done your daily practice. This will keep you focused in the direction of your dreams. Feel free to experiment with different oils as you progress.

Date of Personal AFT Session: _____

[ROUND 1] Step 1 - Set Your Intention/Goal: _____
_____
_____

Rate your intention/goal. How possible does it feel? (Circle One)

    Zero Hope - 0 1 2 3 4 5 6 7 8 9 10 - Absolute Confidence

Step 2 - What does the negative voice say that tells you this is not possible? _____

Step 3 - How do you feel when you hear this negative voice (find ONE word)? _____
Step 4 - Where do you feel this emotion in your body? _____

Step 5 - Drift back to an earlier time when you felt the same way - same emotion in the same place in your body. This memory may appear as a single image or a series of memories, like a movie. You might also have nothing come up. Any of these are okay. Notes on previous memory _____
_____
_____

Step 6 - Smell Memory Release Blend (equal parts YL Lavender, YL Frankincense and YL Stress Away) or other oils - specify which oils used: _____
Step 7 - Notice changes to memory, emotion, bodily sensation: _____
_____
_____

Step 8 - Is there a new belief or mindset that has emerged? _____
_____
_____

Step 9 - Read the original intention/goal and rate it again - how possible does it feel now? (circle one)

    Zero Hope - 0 1 2 3 4 5 6 7 8 9 10 - Absolute Confidence

(If 8 or higher (or if no negative voice), skip to Step 10 - the Affirmation. If less than 8, return to Step 2 on next page.)

How far have you shifted thus far?

Starting Number: _____ New Number: _____

[ROUND 2] Step 2 - What does the inner voice say that tells you this is not possible? _____

Step 3 - How do you feel when you hear this inner voice (find ONE word)? _____

Step 4 - Where do you feel this emotion in your body? _____

Step 5 - Drift back to an earlier time when you felt the same way - same emotion in the same place in your body. This memory may appear as a single image or a series of memories, like a movie. You might also have nothing come up. Any of these are okay. Notes on previous memory _____

Step 6 - Smell YL Inner Child blend or other oils - specify which oils used:

Step 7 - Notice changes to memory, emotion, bodily sensation: _____

Step 8 - Is there a new belief or mindset that has emerged? _____

Step 9 - Read the original intention/goal and rate it again - how possible does it feel now? (circle one)

Zero Hope - 0 1 2 3 4 5 6 7 8 9 10 - Absolute Confidence

(If 8 or higher (or if no negative voice), skip to Step 10 - the Affirmation. If less than 8, return to Step 2 on next page.)

Look how far you've shifted!

Starting Number: _____ Second Number: _____
Third Number: _____

[ROUND 3] Step 2 - What does the inner voice say that tells you this is not possible? _____

_____

Step 3 - How do you feel when you hear this inner voice (find ONE word)? _____

Step 4 - Where do you feel this emotion in your body? _____

_____

Step 5 - Drift back to an earlier time when you felt the same way - same emotion in the same place in your body. This memory may appear as a single image or a series of memories, like a movie. You might also have nothing come up. Any of these are okay. Notes on previous memory _____

_____

_____

Step 6 - Smell YL Release blend or other oils - specify which oils used:

_____

Step 7 - Notice changes to memory, emotion, bodily sensation: _____

_____

_____

Step 8 - Is there a new belief or mindset that has emerged? _____

_____

_____

Step 9 - Read the original intention/goal and rate it again - how possible does it feel now? (circle one)

Zero Hope - 0 1 2 3 4 5 6 7 8 9 10 - Absolute Confidence

Look how far you've shifted!

Starting Number: _____ Second Number: _____
Third Number: _____ Final Number: _____

(Time to set your affirmation, even if you're not yet at an 8 or higher. More shifting will occur during the next 3 steps.)

Step 10 - Affirmation: _____

_____

_____

Step 11 - Stand in Power Pose: Repeat the affirmation for 2 minutes, twice daily, with conviction while standing in a power pose. Smell *Believe*™ or *Transformation*™ Oil Blend as you do this. (You may choose another transforming oil if you'd like, such as *Build Your Dream*™, *Magnify Your Purpose*™, etc) Chosen Oil & Pose: _____

Repeat for *at least three consecutive days*, or until you create a new affirmation. Check off each box when complete.

Always make sure that your energy feels clear when you say the statement. If you experience inner resistance, use the AFT process to identify and release any negative thoughts, feelings, or memories that come up.

Date	AM	PM

Step 12 - Make Your Plan of Action: _____

_____

_____

_____

_____

_____

Follow-up - What has changed in your life because of THIS Aroma Freedom Technique Session? _____

_____

_____

_____

_____

Program your mind daily! As soon as one affirmation is complete or the goal has been reached, create another. Make affirmations a daily habit and soon you will not feel right unless you have done your daily practice. This will keep you focused in the direction of your dreams. Feel free to experiment with different oils as you progress.

Date of Personal AFT Session: _____

[ROUND 1] Step 1 - Set Your Intention/Goal: _____
_____
_____

Rate your intention/goal. How possible does it feel? (Circle One)

    Zero Hope - 0 1 2 3 4 5 6 7 8 9 10 - Absolute Confidence

Step 2 - What does the negative voice say that tells you this is not possible? _____
_____

Step 3 - How do you feel when you hear this negative voice (find ONE word)? _____

Step 4 - Where do you feel this emotion in your body? _____
_____

Step 5 - Drift back to an earlier time when you felt the same way - same emotion in the same place in your body. This memory may appear as a single image or a series of memories, like a movie. You might also have nothing come up. Any of these are okay. Notes on previous memory ____
_____
_____

Step 6 - Smell Memory Release Blend (equal parts YL Lavender, YL Frankincense and YL Stress Away) or other oils - specify which oils used: _____

Step 7 - Notice changes to memory, emotion, bodily sensation: _____
_____
_____

Step 8 - Is there a new belief or mindset that has emerged? _____
_____
_____

Step 9 - Read the original intention/goal and rate it again - how possible does it feel now? (circle one)

    Zero Hope - 0 1 2 3 4 5 6 7 8 9 10 - Absolute Confidence

(If 8 or higher (or if no negative voice), skip to Step 10 - the Affirmation. If less than 8, return to Step 2 on next page.)

How far have you shifted thus far?

Starting Number: _____ New Number: _____

[ROUND 2] Step 2 - What does the inner voice say that tells you this is not possible? _____

_____

Step 3 - How do you feel when you hear this inner voice (find ONE word)? _____

Step 4 - Where do you feel this emotion in your body? _____

Step 5 - Drift back to an earlier time when you felt the same way - same emotion in the same place in your body. This memory may appear as a single image or a series of memories, like a movie. You might also have nothing come up. Any of these are okay. Notes on previous memory _____

_____

Step 6 - Smell YL Inner Child blend or other oils - specify which oils used:

_____

Step 7 - Notice changes to memory, emotion, bodily sensation: _____

_____

Step 8 - Is there a new belief or mindset that has emerged? _____

_____

Step 9 - Read the original intention/goal and rate it again - how possible does it feel now? (circle one)

Zero Hope - 0 1 2 3 4 5 6 7 8 9 10 - Absolute Confidence

(If 8 or higher (or if no negative voice), skip to Step 10 - the Affirmation. If less than 8, return to Step 2 on next page.)

Look how far you've shifted!

Starting Number: _____ Second Number: _____
Third Number: _____

[ROUND 3] Step 2 - What does the inner voice say that tells you this is not possible? _____

_____

Step 3 - How do you feel when you hear this inner voice (find ONE word)? _____

Step 4 - Where do you feel this emotion in your body? _____

_____

Step 5 - Drift back to an earlier time when you felt the same way - same emotion in the same place in your body. This memory may appear as a single image or a series of memories, like a movie. You might also have nothing come up. Any of these are okay. Notes on previous memory _____

_____

Step 6 - Smell YL Release blend or other oils - specify which oils used:

_____

Step 7 - Notice changes to memory, emotion, bodily sensation: _____

_____

Step 8 - Is there a new belief or mindset that has emerged? _____

_____

Step 9 - Read the original intention/goal and rate it again - how possible does it feel now? (circle one)

Zero Hope - 0 1 2 3 4 5 6 7 8 9 10 - Absolute Confidence

Look how far you've shifted!

Starting Number: _____ Second Number: _____
Third Number: _____ Final Number: _____

(Time to set your affirmation, even if you're not yet at an 8 or higher. More shifting will occur during the next 3 steps.)

Step 10 - Affirmation: _____

_____

_____

Step 11 - Stand in Power Pose: Repeat the affirmation for 2 minutes, twice daily, with conviction while standing in a power pose. Smell *Believe™* or *Transformation™* Oil Blend as you do this. (You may choose another transforming oil if you'd like, such as *Build Your Dream™*, *Magnify Your Purpose™*, etc) Chosen Oil & Pose: _____

Repeat for *at least three consecutive days,* or until you create a new affirmation. Check off each box when complete.

Always make sure that your energy feels clear when you say the statement. If you experience inner resistance, use the AFT process to identify and release any negative thoughts, feelings, or memories that come up.

Date	AM	PM

Step 12 - Make Your Plan of Action: _____

_____

_____

_____

_____

_____

Follow-up - What has changed in your life because of THIS Aroma Freedom Technique Session? _____

_____

_____

_____

_____

Program your mind daily! As soon as one affirmation is complete or the goal has been reached, create another. Make affirmations a daily habit and soon you will not feel right unless you have done your daily practice. This will keep you focused in the direction of your dreams. Feel free to experiment with different oils as you progress.

Date of Personal AFT Session: _____

[ROUND 1] Step 1 - Set Your Intention/Goal: _____
_____
_____

Rate your intention/goal. How possible does it feel? (Circle One)

    Zero Hope - 0 1 2 3 4 5 6 7 8 9 10 - Absolute Confidence

Step 2 - What does the negative voice say that tells you this is not possible? _____
_____

Step 3 - How do you feel when you hear this negative voice (find ONE word)? _____

Step 4 - Where do you feel this emotion in your body? _____
_____

Step 5 - Drift back to an earlier time when you felt the same way - same emotion in the same place in your body. This memory may appear as a single image or a series of memories, like a movie. You might also have nothing come up. Any of these are okay. Notes on previous memory _____
_____
_____

Step 6 - Smell Memory Release Blend (equal parts YL Lavender, YL Frankincense and YL Stress Away) or other oils - specify which oils used: _____

Step 7 - Notice changes to memory, emotion, bodily sensation: _____
_____

Step 8 - Is there a new belief or mindset that has emerged? _____
_____

Step 9 - Read the original intention/goal and rate it again - how possible does it feel now? (circle one)

    Zero Hope - 0 1 2 3 4 5 6 7 8 9 10 - Absolute Confidence

(If 8 or higher (or if no negative voice), skip to Step 10 - the Affirmation. If less than 8, return to Step 2 on next page.)

How far have you shifted thus far?

Starting Number: _____ New Number: _____

[ROUND 2] Step 2 - What does the inner voice say that tells you this is not possible? _____

_____

Step 3 - How do you feel when you hear this inner voice (find ONE word)? _____

Step 4 - Where do you feel this emotion in your body? _____

_____

Step 5 - Drift back to an earlier time when you felt the same way - same emotion in the same place in your body. This memory may appear as a single image or a series of memories, like a movie. You might also have nothing come up. Any of these are okay. Notes on previous memory _____

_____

_____

Step 6 - Smell YL Inner Child blend or other oils - specify which oils used:

_____

Step 7 - Notice changes to memory, emotion, bodily sensation: _____

_____

_____

Step 8 - Is there a new belief or mindset that has emerged? _____

_____

_____

Step 9 - Read the original intention/goal and rate it again - how possible does it feel now? (circle one)

Zero Hope - 0 1 2 3 4 5 6 7 8 9 10 - Absolute Confidence

(If 8 or higher (or if no negative voice), skip to Step 10 - the Affirmation. If less than 8, return to Step 2 on next page.)

Look how far you've shifted!

Starting Number: _____ Second Number: _____

Third Number: _____

[ROUND 3] Step 2 - What does the inner voice say that tells you this is not possible? _____

_____

Step 3 - How do you feel when you hear this inner voice (find ONE word)? _____

Step 4 - Where do you feel this emotion in your body? _____

_____

Step 5 - Drift back to an earlier time when you felt the same way - same emotion in the same place in your body. This memory may appear as a single image or a series of memories, like a movie. You might also have nothing come up. Any of these are okay. Notes on previous memory ____

_____
_____

Step 6 - Smell YL Release blend or other oils - specify which oils used:

_____

Step 7 - Notice changes to memory, emotion, bodily sensation: _____

_____
_____

Step 8 - Is there a new belief or mindset that has emerged? _____

_____
_____

Step 9 - Read the original intention/goal and rate it again - how possible does it feel now? (circle one)

Zero Hope - 0 1 2 3 4 5 6 7 8 9 10 - Absolute Confidence

Look how far you've shifted!

Starting Number: _____ Second Number: _____
Third Number: _____ Final Number: _____

(Time to set your affirmation, even if you're not yet at an 8 or higher. More shifting will occur during the next 3 steps.)

Step 10 - Affirmation: _____

_____
_____

Step 11 - Stand in Power Pose: Repeat the affirmation for 2 minutes, twice daily, with conviction while standing in a power pose. Smell *Believe*™ or *Transformation*™ Oil Blend as you do this. (You may choose another transforming oil if you'd like, such as *Build Your Dream*™, *Magnify Your Purpose*™, etc) Chosen Oil & Pose: _____

Repeat for *at least three consecutive days*, or until you create a new affirmation. Check off each box when complete.

Always make sure that your energy feels clear when you say the statement. If you experience inner resistance, use the AFT process to identify and release any negative thoughts, feelings, or memories that come up.

Date	AM	PM

Step 12 - Make Your Plan of Action: _____

_____

_____

_____

_____

_____

Follow-up - What has changed in your life because of THIS Aroma Freedom Technique Session? _____

_____

_____

_____

_____

Program your mind daily! As soon as one affirmation is complete or the goal has been reached, create another. Make affirmations a daily habit and soon you will not feel right unless you have done your daily practice. This will keep you focused in the direction of your dreams. Feel free to experiment with different oils as you progress.

Date of Personal AFT Session: _____

[ROUND 1] Step 1 - Set Your Intention/Goal: _____

_____

_____

Rate your intention/goal. How possible does it feel? (Circle One)

Zero Hope - 0 1 2 3 4 5 6 7 8 9 10 - Absolute Confidence

Step 2 - What does the negative voice say that tells you this is not possible? _____

_____

Step 3 - How do you feel when you hear this negative voice (find ONE word)? _____

Step 4 - Where do you feel this emotion in your body? _____

_____

Step 5 - Drift back to an earlier time when you felt the same way - same emotion in the same place in your body. This memory may appear as a single image or a series of memories, like a movie. You might also have nothing come up. Any of these are okay. Notes on previous memory ____

_____

_____

Step 6 - Smell Memory Release Blend (equal parts YL Lavender, YL Frankincense and YL Stress Away) or other oils - specify which oils used: _____

Step 7 - Notice changes to memory, emotion, bodily sensation: _____

_____

_____

Step 8 - Is there a new belief or mindset that has emerged? _____

_____

_____

Step 9 - Read the original intention/goal and rate it again - how possible does it feel now? (circle one)

Zero Hope - 0 1 2 3 4 5 6 7 8 9 10 - Absolute Confidence

(If 8 or higher (or if no negative voice), skip to Step 10 - the Affirmation. If less than 8, return to Step 2 on next page.)

How far have you shifted thus far?

Starting Number: _____ New Number: _____

[ROUND 2] Step 2 - What does the inner voice say that tells you this is not possible? _____
_____

Step 3 - How do you feel when you hear this inner voice (find ONE word)? _____

Step 4 - Where do you feel this emotion in your body? _____
_____

Step 5 - Drift back to an earlier time when you felt the same way - same emotion in the same place in your body. This memory may appear as a single image or a series of memories, like a movie. You might also have nothing come up. Any of these are okay. Notes on previous memory _____
_____
_____

Step 6 - Smell YL Inner Child blend or other oils - specify which oils used:
_____

Step 7 - Notice changes to memory, emotion, bodily sensation: _____
_____
_____

Step 8 - Is there a new belief or mindset that has emerged? _____
_____

Step 9 - Read the original intention/goal and rate it again - how possible does it feel now? (circle one)

Zero Hope - 0 1 2 3 4 5 6 7 8 9 10 - Absolute Confidence

(If 8 or higher (or if no negative voice), skip to Step 10 - the Affirmation. If less than 8, return to Step 2 on next page.)

Look how far you've shifted!

Starting Number: _____ Second Number: _____
Third Number: _____

[ROUND 3] Step 2 - What does the inner voice say that tells you this is not possible? _____

_____

Step 3 - How do you feel when you hear this inner voice (find ONE word)? _____

Step 4 - Where do you feel this emotion in your body? _____

_____

Step 5 - Drift back to an earlier time when you felt the same way - same emotion in the same place in your body. This memory may appear as a single image or a series of memories, like a movie. You might also have nothing come up. Any of these are okay. Notes on previous memory _____

_____

_____

Step 6 - Smell YL Release blend or other oils - specify which oils used:

_____

Step 7 - Notice changes to memory, emotion, bodily sensation: _____

_____

_____

Step 8 - Is there a new belief or mindset that has emerged? _____

_____

_____

Step 9 - Read the original intention/goal and rate it again - how possible does it feel now? (circle one)

Zero Hope - 0 1 2 3 4 5 6 7 8 9 10 - Absolute Confidence

Look how far you've shifted!

Starting Number: _____ Second Number: _____
Third Number: _____ Final Number: _____

(Time to set your affirmation, even if you're not yet at an 8 or higher. More shifting will occur during the next 3 steps.)

Step 10 - Affirmation: _____

_____

_____

Step 11 - Stand in Power Pose: Repeat the affirmation for 2 minutes, twice daily, with conviction while standing in a power pose. Smell *Believe™* or *Transformation™* Oil Blend as you do this. (You may choose another transforming oil if you'd like, such as *Build Your Dream™*, *Magnify Your Purpose™*, etc) Chosen Oil & Pose: _____

Repeat for *at least three consecutive days*, or until you create a new affirmation. Check off each box when complete.

Always make sure that your energy feels clear when you say the statement. If you experience inner resistance, use the AFT process to identify and release any negative thoughts, feelings, or memories that come up.

Date	AM	PM

Step 12 - Make Your Plan of Action: _____

_____
_____
_____
_____
_____

Follow-up - What has changed in your life because of THIS Aroma Freedom Technique Session? _____

_____
_____
_____
_____

Program your mind daily! As soon as one affirmation is complete or the goal has been reached, create another. Make affirmations a daily habit and soon you will not feel right unless you have done your daily practice. This will keep you focused in the direction of your dreams. Feel free to experiment with different oils as you progress.

Date of Personal AFT Session: _____

[ROUND 1] Step 1 - Set Your Intention/Goal: _____

_____
_____

Rate your intention/goal. How possible does it feel? (Circle One)

Zero Hope - 0 1 2 3 4 5 6 7 8 9 10 - Absolute Confidence

Step 2 - What does the negative voice say that tells you this is not possible? _____

Step 3 - How do you feel when you hear this negative voice (find ONE word)? _____

Step 4 - Where do you feel this emotion in your body? _____

_____

Step 5 - Drift back to an earlier time when you felt the same way - same emotion in the same place in your body. This memory may appear as a single image or a series of memories, like a movie. You might also have nothing come up. Any of these are okay. Notes on previous memory _____

_____
_____

Step 6 - Smell Memory Release Blend (equal parts YL Lavender, YL Frankincense and YL Stress Away) or other oils - specify which oils used: _____

Step 7 - Notice changes to memory, emotion, bodily sensation: _____

_____
_____

Step 8 - Is there a new belief or mindset that has emerged? _____

_____
_____

Step 9 - Read the original intention/goal and rate it again - how possible does it feel now? (circle one)

Zero Hope - 0 1 2 3 4 5 6 7 8 9 10 - Absolute Confidence

(If 8 or higher (or if no negative voice), skip to Step 10 - the Affirmation. If less than 8, return to Step 2 on next page.)

How far have you shifted thus far?

Starting Number: _____ New Number: _____

[ROUND 2] Step 2 - What does the inner voice say that tells you this is not possible? _____

_____

Step 3 - How do you feel when you hear this inner voice (find ONE word)? _____

Step 4 - Where do you feel this emotion in your body? _____

_____

Step 5 - Drift back to an earlier time when you felt the same way - same emotion in the same place in your body. This memory may appear as a single image or a series of memories, like a movie. You might also have nothing come up. Any of these are okay. Notes on previous memory _____

_____

_____

Step 6 - Smell YL Inner Child blend or other oils - specify which oils used:

_____

Step 7 - Notice changes to memory, emotion, bodily sensation: _____

_____

_____

Step 8 - Is there a new belief or mindset that has emerged? _____

_____

Step 9 - Read the original intention/goal and rate it again - how possible does it feel now? (circle one)

Zero Hope - 0 1 2 3 4 5 6 7 8 9 10 - Absolute Confidence

(If 8 or higher (or if no negative voice), skip to Step 10 - the Affirmation. If less than 8, return to Step 2 on next page.)

Look how far you've shifted!

Starting Number: _____ Second Number: _____
Third Number: _____

[ROUND 3] Step 2 - What does the inner voice say that tells you this is not possible? _____

Step 3 - How do you feel when you hear this inner voice (find ONE word)? _____

Step 4 - Where do you feel this emotion in your body? _____

Step 5 - Drift back to an earlier time when you felt the same way - same emotion in the same place in your body. This memory may appear as a single image or a series of memories, like a movie. You might also have nothing come up. Any of these are okay. Notes on previous memory _____
_____

Step 6 - Smell YL Release blend or other oils - specify which oils used:
_____

Step 7 - Notice changes to memory, emotion, bodily sensation: _____
_____

Step 8 - Is there a new belief or mindset that has emerged? _____
_____

Step 9 - Read the original intention/goal and rate it again - how possible does it feel now? (circle one)

Zero Hope - 0 1 2 3 4 5 6 7 8 9 10 - Absolute Confidence

Look how far you've shifted!

Starting Number: _____ Second Number: _____
Third Number: _____ Final Number: _____

(Time to set your affirmation, even if you're not yet at an 8 or higher. More shifting will occur during the next 3 steps.)

Step 10 - Affirmation: _____
_____
_____

Step 11 - Stand in Power Pose: Repeat the affirmation for 2 minutes, twice daily, with conviction while standing in a power pose. Smell *Believe*™ or *Transformation*™ Oil Blend as you do this. (You may choose another transforming oil if you'd like, such as *Build Your Dream*™, *Magnify Your Purpose*™, etc) Chosen Oil & Pose: _____

Repeat for *at least three consecutive days*, or until you create a new affirmation. Check off each box when complete.

Always make sure that your energy feels clear when you say the statement. If you experience inner resistance, use the AFT process to identify and release any negative thoughts, feelings, or memories that come up.

Date	AM	PM

Step 12 - Make Your Plan of Action: _____

_____

_____

_____

_____

_____

Follow-up - What has changed in your life because of THIS Aroma Freedom Technique Session? _____

_____

_____

_____

_____

Program your mind daily! As soon as one affirmation is complete or the goal has been reached, create another. Make affirmations a daily habit and soon you will not feel right unless you have done your daily practice. This will keep you focused in the direction of your dreams. Feel free to experiment with different oils as you progress.

Date of Personal AFT Session: _____

[ROUND 1] Step 1 - Set Your Intention/Goal: _____

_____

Rate your intention/goal. How possible does it feel? (Circle One)

    Zero Hope - 0 1 2 3 4 5 6 7 8 9 10 - Absolute Confidence

Step 2 - What does the negative voice say that tells you this is not possible? _____

_____

Step 3 - How do you feel when you hear this negative voice (find ONE word)? _____

Step 4 - Where do you feel this emotion in your body? _____

_____

Step 5 - Drift back to an earlier time when you felt the same way - same emotion in the same place in your body. This memory may appear as a single image or a series of memories, like a movie. You might also have nothing come up. Any of these are okay. Notes on previous memory ____

_____

Step 6 - Smell Memory Release Blend (equal parts YL Lavender, YL Frankincense and YL Stress Away) or other oils - specify which oils used: _____

Step 7 - Notice changes to memory, emotion, bodily sensation: _____

_____

Step 8 - Is there a new belief or mindset that has emerged? _____

_____

Step 9 - Read the original intention/goal and rate it again - how possible does it feel now? (circle one)

    Zero Hope - 0 1 2 3 4 5 6 7 8 9 10 - Absolute Confidence

(If 8 or higher (or if no negative voice), skip to Step 10 - the Affirmation. If less than 8, return to Step 2 on next page.)

How far have you shifted thus far?

Starting Number: _____ New Number: _____

[ROUND 2] Step 2 - What does the inner voice say that tells you this is not possible? _____

_____

Step 3 - How do you feel when you hear this inner voice (find ONE word)? _____

Step 4 - Where do you feel this emotion in your body? _____

_____

Step 5 - Drift back to an earlier time when you felt the same way - same emotion in the same place in your body. This memory may appear as a single image or a series of memories, like a movie. You might also have nothing come up. Any of these are okay. Notes on previous memory _____

_____

_____

Step 6 - Smell YL Inner Child blend or other oils - specify which oils used:

_____

Step 7 - Notice changes to memory, emotion, bodily sensation: _____

_____

_____

Step 8 - Is there a new belief or mindset that has emerged? _____

_____

_____

Step 9 - Read the original intention/goal and rate it again - how possible does it feel now? (circle one)

Zero Hope - 0 1 2 3 4 5 6 7 8 9 10 - Absolute Confidence

(If 8 or higher (or if no negative voice), skip to Step 10 - the Affirmation. If less than 8, return to Step 2 on next page.)

Look how far you've shifted!

Starting Number: _____ Second Number: _____
Third Number: _____

[ROUND 3] Step 2 - What does the inner voice say that tells you this is not possible? _____

_____

Step 3 - How do you feel when you hear this inner voice (find ONE word)? _____

Step 4 - Where do you feel this emotion in your body? _____

_____

Step 5 - Drift back to an earlier time when you felt the same way - same emotion in the same place in your body. This memory may appear as a single image or a series of memories, like a movie. You might also have nothing come up. Any of these are okay. Notes on previous memory _____

_____

Step 6 - Smell YL Release blend or other oils - specify which oils used:

_____

Step 7 - Notice changes to memory, emotion, bodily sensation: _____

_____

Step 8 - Is there a new belief or mindset that has emerged? _____

_____

Step 9 - Read the original intention/goal and rate it again - how possible does it feel now? (circle one)

Zero Hope - 0 1 2 3 4 5 6 7 8 9 10 - Absolute Confidence

Look how far you've shifted!

Starting Number: _____ Second Number: _____
Third Number: _____ Final Number: _____

(Time to set your affirmation, even if you're not yet at an 8 or higher. More shifting will occur during the next 3 steps.)

Step 10 - Affirmation: _____

_____

_____

Step 11 - Stand in Power Pose: Repeat the affirmation for 2 minutes, twice daily, with conviction while standing in a power pose. Smell *Believe*™ or *Transformation*™ Oil Blend as you do this. (You may choose another transforming oil if you'd like, such as *Build Your Dream*™, *Magnify Your Purpose*™, etc) Chosen Oil & Pose: _____

Repeat for *at least three consecutive days*, or until you create a new affirmation. Check off each box when complete.

Always make sure that your energy feels clear when you say the statement. If you experience inner resistance, use the AFT process to identify and release any negative thoughts, feelings, or memories that come up.

Date	AM	PM

Step 12 - Make Your Plan of Action: _____

_____

_____

_____

_____

_____

Follow-up - What has changed in your life because of THIS Aroma Freedom Technique Session? _____

_____

_____

_____

_____

Program your mind daily! As soon as one affirmation is complete or the goal has been reached, create another. Make affirmations a daily habit and soon you will not feel right unless you have done your daily practice. This will keep you focused in the direction of your dreams. Feel free to experiment with different oils as you progress.

Date of Personal AFT Session: _____

[ROUND 1] Step 1 - Set Your Intention/Goal: _____
_____
_____

Rate your intention/goal. How possible does it feel? (Circle One)

Zero Hope - 0 1 2 3 4 5 6 7 8 9 10 - Absolute Confidence

Step 2 - What does the negative voice say that tells you this is not possible? _____
_____

Step 3 - How do you feel when you hear this negative voice (find ONE word)? _____
Step 4 - Where do you feel this emotion in your body? _____
_____

Step 5 - Drift back to an earlier time when you felt the same way - same emotion in the same place in your body. This memory may appear as a single image or a series of memories, like a movie. You might also have nothing come up. Any of these are okay. Notes on previous memory ____
_____
_____

Step 6 - Smell Memory Release Blend (equal parts YL Lavender, YL Frankincense and YL Stress Away) or other oils - specify which oils used: _____
Step 7 - Notice changes to memory, emotion, bodily sensation: _____
_____

Step 8 - Is there a new belief or mindset that has emerged? _____
_____

Step 9 - Read the original intention/goal and rate it again - how possible does it feel now? (circle one)

Zero Hope - 0 1 2 3 4 5 6 7 8 9 10 - Absolute Confidence

(If 8 or higher (or if no negative voice), skip to Step 10 - the Affirmation. If less than 8, return to Step 2 on next page.)

How far have you shifted thus far?

Starting Number: _____ New Number: _____

[ROUND 2] Step 2 - What does the inner voice say that tells you this is not possible? _____

_____

Step 3 - How do you feel when you hear this inner voice (find ONE word)? _____

Step 4 - Where do you feel this emotion in your body? _____

_____

Step 5 - Drift back to an earlier time when you felt the same way - same emotion in the same place in your body. This memory may appear as a single image or a series of memories, like a movie. You might also have nothing come up. Any of these are okay. Notes on previous memory _____

_____

_____

Step 6 - Smell YL Inner Child blend or other oils - specify which oils used:

_____

Step 7 - Notice changes to memory, emotion, bodily sensation: _____

_____

_____

Step 8 - Is there a new belief or mindset that has emerged? _____

_____

_____

Step 9 - Read the original intention/goal and rate it again - how possible does it feel now? (circle one)

Zero Hope - 0 1 2 3 4 5 6 7 8 9 10 - Absolute Confidence

(If 8 or higher (or if no negative voice), skip to Step 10 - the Affirmation. If less than 8, return to Step 2 on next page.)

Look how far you've shifted!

Starting Number: _____ Second Number: _____
Third Number: _____

[ROUND 3] Step 2 - What does the inner voice say that tells you this is not possible? _____

Step 3 - How do you feel when you hear this inner voice (find ONE word)? _____
Step 4 - Where do you feel this emotion in your body? _____

Step 5 - Drift back to an earlier time when you felt the same way - same emotion in the same place in your body. This memory may appear as a single image or a series of memories, like a movie. You might also have nothing come up. Any of these are okay. Notes on previous memory _____
_____
_____

Step 6 - Smell YL Release blend or other oils - specify which oils used:
_____

Step 7 - Notice changes to memory, emotion, bodily sensation: _____
_____
_____

Step 8 - Is there a new belief or mindset that has emerged? _____
_____
_____

Step 9 - Read the original intention/goal and rate it again - how possible does it feel now? (circle one)

Zero Hope - 0 1 2 3 4 5 6 7 8 9 10 - Absolute Confidence

Look how far you've shifted!

Starting Number: _____ Second Number: _____
Third Number: _____ Final Number: _____

(Time to set your affirmation, even if you're not yet at an 8 or higher. More shifting will occur during the next 3 steps.)

Step 10 - Affirmation: _____
_____
_____

Step 11 - Stand in Power Pose: Repeat the affirmation for 2 minutes, twice daily, with conviction while standing in a power pose. Smell *Believe*™ or *Transformation*™ Oil Blend as you do this. (You may choose another transforming oil if you'd like, such as *Build Your Dream*™, *Magnify Your Purpose*™, etc) Chosen Oil & Pose: _____

Repeat for *at least three consecutive days*, or until you create a new affirmation. Check off each box when complete.

Always make sure that your energy feels clear when you say the statement. If you experience inner resistance, use the AFT process to identify and release any negative thoughts, feelings, or memories that come up.

Date	AM	PM

Step 12 - Make Your Plan of Action: _____

_____

_____

_____

_____

_____

Follow-up - What has changed in your life because of THIS Aroma Freedom Technique Session? _____

_____

_____

_____

_____

Program your mind daily! As soon as one affirmation is complete or the goal has been reached, create another. Make affirmations a daily habit and soon you will not feel right unless you have done your daily practice. This will keep you focused in the direction of your dreams. Feel free to experiment with different oils as you progress.

Date of Personal AFT Session: _____

[ROUND 1] Step 1 - Set Your Intention/Goal: _____
_____
_____

Rate your intention/goal. How possible does it feel? (Circle One)

    Zero Hope - 0 1 2 3 4 5 6 7 8 9 10 - Absolute Confidence

Step 2 - What does the negative voice say that tells you this is not possible? _____
_____

Step 3 - How do you feel when you hear this negative voice (find ONE word)? _____

Step 4 - Where do you feel this emotion in your body? _____
_____

Step 5 - Drift back to an earlier time when you felt the same way - same emotion in the same place in your body. This memory may appear as a single image or a series of memories, like a movie. You might also have nothing come up. Any of these are okay. Notes on previous memory _____
_____
_____

Step 6 - Smell Memory Release Blend (equal parts YL Lavender, YL Frankincense and YL Stress Away) or other oils - specify which oils used: _____

Step 7 - Notice changes to memory, emotion, bodily sensation: _____
_____
_____

Step 8 - Is there a new belief or mindset that has emerged? _____
_____
_____

Step 9 - Read the original intention/goal and rate it again - how possible does it feel now? (circle one)

    Zero Hope - 0 1 2 3 4 5 6 7 8 9 10 - Absolute Confidence

(If 8 or higher (or if no negative voice), skip to Step 10 - the Affirmation. If less than 8, return to Step 2 on next page.)

How far have you shifted thus far?

Starting Number: _____ New Number: _____

[ROUND 2] Step 2 - What does the inner voice say that tells you this is not possible? _____

_____

Step 3 - How do you feel when you hear this inner voice (find ONE word)? _____

Step 4 - Where do you feel this emotion in your body? _____

_____

Step 5 - Drift back to an earlier time when you felt the same way - same emotion in the same place in your body. This memory may appear as a single image or a series of memories, like a movie. You might also have nothing come up. Any of these are okay. Notes on previous memory _____

_____

_____

Step 6 - Smell YL Inner Child blend or other oils - specify which oils used:

_____

Step 7 - Notice changes to memory, emotion, bodily sensation: _____

_____

_____

Step 8 - Is there a new belief or mindset that has emerged? _____

_____

_____

Step 9 - Read the original intention/goal and rate it again - how possible does it feel now? (circle one)

Zero Hope - 0 1 2 3 4 5 6 7 8 9 10 - Absolute Confidence

(If 8 or higher (or if no negative voice), skip to Step 10 - the Affirmation. If less than 8, return to Step 2 on next page.)

Look how far you've shifted!

Starting Number: _____ Second Number: _____
Third Number: _____

[ROUND 3] Step 2 - What does the inner voice say that tells you this is not possible? _____

_____

Step 3 - How do you feel when you hear this inner voice (find ONE word)? _____

Step 4 - Where do you feel this emotion in your body? _____

_____

Step 5 - Drift back to an earlier time when you felt the same way - same emotion in the same place in your body. This memory may appear as a single image or a series of memories, like a movie. You might also have nothing come up. Any of these are okay. Notes on previous memory _____

_____

_____

Step 6 - Smell YL Release blend or other oils - specify which oils used:

_____

Step 7 - Notice changes to memory, emotion, bodily sensation: _____

_____

_____

Step 8 - Is there a new belief or mindset that has emerged? _____

_____

_____

Step 9 - Read the original intention/goal and rate it again - how possible does it feel now? (circle one)

Zero Hope - 0 1 2 3 4 5 6 7 8 9 10 - Absolute Confidence

Look how far you've shifted!

Starting Number: _____ Second Number: _____
Third Number: _____ Final Number: _____

(Time to set your affirmation, even if you're not yet at an 8 or higher. More shifting will occur during the next 3 steps.)

Step 10 - Affirmation: _____

_____

_____

Step 11 - Stand in Power Pose: Repeat the affirmation for 2 minutes, twice daily, with conviction while standing in a power pose. Smell *Believe*™ or *Transformation*™ Oil Blend as you do this. (You may choose another transforming oil if you'd like, such as *Build Your Dream*™, *Magnify Your Purpose*™, etc) Chosen Oil & Pose: _____

Repeat for *at least three consecutive days,* or until you create a new affirmation. Check off each box when complete.

Always make sure that your energy feels clear when you say the statement. If you experience inner resistance, use the AFT process to identify and release any negative thoughts, feelings, or memories that come up.

Date	AM	PM

Step 12 - Make Your Plan of Action: _____

_____

_____

_____

_____

_____

Follow-up - What has changed in your life because of THIS Aroma Freedom Technique Session? _____

_____

_____

_____

_____

Program your mind daily! As soon as one affirmation is complete or the goal has been reached, create another. Make affirmations a daily habit and soon you will not feel right unless you have done your daily practice. This will keep you focused in the direction of your dreams. Feel free to experiment with different oils as you progress.

Date of Personal AFT Session: _____

[ROUND 1] Step 1 - Set Your Intention/Goal: _____
_____
_____

Rate your intention/goal. How possible does it feel? (Circle One)

Zero Hope - 0 1 2 3 4 5 6 7 8 9 10 - Absolute Confidence

Step 2 - What does the negative voice say that tells you this is not possible? _____
_____

Step 3 - How do you feel when you hear this negative voice (find ONE word)? _____

Step 4 - Where do you feel this emotion in your body? _____

Step 5 - Drift back to an earlier time when you felt the same way - same emotion in the same place in your body. This memory may appear as a single image or a series of memories, like a movie. You might also have nothing come up. Any of these are okay. Notes on previous memory _____
_____
_____

Step 6 - Smell Memory Release Blend (equal parts YL Lavender, YL Frankincense and YL Stress Away) or other oils - specify which oils used: _____

Step 7 - Notice changes to memory, emotion, bodily sensation: _____
_____
_____

Step 8 - Is there a new belief or mindset that has emerged? _____
_____
_____

Step 9 - Read the original intention/goal and rate it again - how possible does it feel now? (circle one)

Zero Hope - 0 1 2 3 4 5 6 7 8 9 10 - Absolute Confidence

(If 8 or higher (or if no negative voice), skip to Step 10 - the Affirmation. If less than 8, return to Step 2 on next page.)

How far have you shifted thus far?

Starting Number: _____ New Number: _____

[ROUND 2] Step 2 - What does the inner voice say that tells you this is not possible? _____

_____

Step 3 - How do you feel when you hear this inner voice (find ONE word)? _____

Step 4 - Where do you feel this emotion in your body? _____

Step 5 - Drift back to an earlier time when you felt the same way - same emotion in the same place in your body. This memory may appear as a single image or a series of memories, like a movie. You might also have nothing come up. Any of these are okay. Notes on previous memory _____

_____

_____

Step 6 - Smell YL Inner Child blend or other oils - specify which oils used:

_____

Step 7 - Notice changes to memory, emotion, bodily sensation: _____

_____

_____

Step 8 - Is there a new belief or mindset that has emerged? _____

_____

_____

Step 9 - Read the original intention/goal and rate it again - how possible does it feel now? (circle one)

Zero Hope - 0 1 2 3 4 5 6 7 8 9 10 - Absolute Confidence

(If 8 or higher (or if no negative voice), skip to Step 10 - the Affirmation. If less than 8, return to Step 2 on next page.)

Look how far you've shifted!

Starting Number: _____ Second Number: _____

Third Number: _____

[ROUND 3] Step 2 - What does the inner voice say that tells you this is not possible? _____

_____

Step 3 - How do you feel when you hear this inner voice (find ONE word)? _____

Step 4 - Where do you feel this emotion in your body? _____

_____

Step 5 - Drift back to an earlier time when you felt the same way - same emotion in the same place in your body. This memory may appear as a single image or a series of memories, like a movie. You might also have nothing come up. Any of these are okay. Notes on previous memory _____

_____

Step 6 - Smell YL Release blend or other oils - specify which oils used:

_____

Step 7 - Notice changes to memory, emotion, bodily sensation: _____

_____

Step 8 - Is there a new belief or mindset that has emerged? _____

_____

Step 9 - Read the original intention/goal and rate it again - how possible does it feel now? (circle one)

Zero Hope - 0 1 2 3 4 5 6 7 8 9 10 - Absolute Confidence

Look how far you've shifted!

Starting Number: _____ Second Number: _____
Third Number: _____ Final Number: _____

(Time to set your affirmation, even if you're not yet at an 8 or higher. More shifting will occur during the next 3 steps.)

Step 10 - Affirmation: _____

_____

_____

Step 11 - Stand in Power Pose: Repeat the affirmation for 2 minutes, twice daily, with conviction while standing in a power pose. Smell *Believe*™ or *Transformation*™ Oil Blend as you do this. (You may choose another transforming oil if you'd like, such as *Build Your Dream*™, *Magnify Your Purpose*™, etc) Chosen Oil & Pose: _____

Repeat for *at least three consecutive days*, or until you create a new affirmation. Check off each box when complete.

Always make sure that your energy feels clear when you say the statement. If you experience inner resistance, use the AFT process to identify and release any negative thoughts, feelings, or memories that come up.

Date	AM	PM

Step 12 - Make Your Plan of Action: _____

_____

_____

_____

_____

_____

Follow-up - What has changed in your life because of THIS Aroma Freedom Technique Session? _____

_____

_____

_____

_____

Program your mind daily! As soon as one affirmation is complete or the goal has been reached, create another. Make affirmations a daily habit and soon you will not feel right unless you have done your daily practice. This will keep you focused in the direction of your dreams. Feel free to experiment with different oils as you progress.

Date of Personal AFT Session: _____

[ROUND 1] Step 1 - Set Your Intention/Goal: _____
_____
_____

Rate your intention/goal. How possible does it feel? (Circle One)

    Zero Hope - 0 1 2 3 4 5 6 7 8 9 10 - Absolute Confidence

**Step 2 - What does the negative voice say that tells you this is not
possible?** _____
_____

**Step 3 - How do you feel when you hear this negative voice (find ONE
word)?** _____

Step 4 - Where do you feel this emotion in your body? _____

_____

**Step 5 - Drift back to an earlier time when you felt the same way - same
emotion in the same place in your body. This memory may appear as a
single image or a series of memories, like a movie. You might also have
nothing come up. Any of these are okay.** Notes on previous memory _____
_____
_____

**Step 6 - Smell Memory Release Blend (equal parts YL Lavender, YL
Frankincense and YL Stress Away) or other oils - specify which oils
used:** _____

Step 7 - Notice changes to memory, emotion, bodily sensation: _____
_____
_____

Step 8 - Is there a new belief or mindset that has emerged? _____
_____
_____

**Step 9 - Read the original intention/goal and rate it again - how possible
does it feel now? (circle one)**

    Zero Hope - 0 1 2 3 4 5 6 7 8 9 10 - Absolute Confidence

(If 8 or higher (or if no negative voice), skip to Step 10 - the Affirmation. If less than
8, return to Step 2 on next page.)

How far have you shifted thus far?

Starting Number: _____ New Number: _____

[ROUND 2] Step 2 - What does the inner voice say that tells you this is not possible? _____

_____

Step 3 - How do you feel when you hear this inner voice (find ONE word)? _____

Step 4 - Where do you feel this emotion in your body? _____

Step 5 - Drift back to an earlier time when you felt the same way - same emotion in the same place in your body. This memory may appear as a single image or a series of memories, like a movie. You might also have nothing come up. Any of these are okay. Notes on previous memory _____

_____

_____

Step 6 - Smell YL Inner Child blend or other oils - specify which oils used:

_____

Step 7 - Notice changes to memory, emotion, bodily sensation: _____

_____

_____

Step 8 - Is there a new belief or mindset that has emerged? _____

_____

_____

Step 9 - Read the original intention/goal and rate it again - how possible does it feel now? (circle one)

Zero Hope - 0 1 2 3 4 5 6 7 8 9 10 - Absolute Confidence

(If 8 or higher (or if no negative voice), skip to Step 10 - the Affirmation. If less than 8, return to Step 2 on next page.)

Look how far you've shifted!

Starting Number: _____ Second Number: _____
Third Number: _____

[ROUND 3] Step 2 - What does the inner voice say that tells you this is not possible? _____

Step 3 - How do you feel when you hear this inner voice (find ONE word)? _____

Step 4 - Where do you feel this emotion in your body? _____

Step 5 - Drift back to an earlier time when you felt the same way - same emotion in the same place in your body. This memory may appear as a single image or a series of memories, like a movie. You might also have nothing come up. Any of these are okay. Notes on previous memory ____

_____
_____

Step 6 - Smell YL Release blend or other oils - specify which oils used:
_____

Step 7 - Notice changes to memory, emotion, bodily sensation: _____

_____
_____

Step 8 - Is there a new belief or mindset that has emerged? _____

_____
_____

Step 9 - Read the original intention/goal and rate it again - how possible does it feel now? (circle one)

Zero Hope - 0 1 2 3 4 5 6 7 8 9 10 - Absolute Confidence

Look how far you've shifted!

Starting Number: _____ Second Number: _____
Third Number: _____ Final Number: _____

(Time to set your affirmation, even if you're not yet at an 8 or higher. More shifting will occur during the next 3 steps.)

Step 10 - Affirmation: _____

_____
_____

Step 11 - Stand in Power Pose: Repeat the affirmation for 2 minutes, twice daily, with conviction while standing in a power pose. Smell *Believe*™ or *Transformation*™ Oil Blend as you do this. (You may choose another transforming oil if you'd like, such as *Build Your Dream*™, *Magnify Your Purpose*™, etc) Chosen Oil & Pose: _____

Repeat for *at least three consecutive days*, or until you create a new affirmation. Check off each box when complete.

Always make sure that your energy feels clear when you say the statement. If you experience inner resistance, use the AFT process to identify and release any negative thoughts, feelings, or memories that come up.

Date	AM	PM

Step 12 - Make Your Plan of Action: _____

_____

_____

_____

_____

_____

Follow-up - What has changed in your life because of THIS Aroma Freedom Technique Session? _____

_____

_____

_____

_____

Program your mind daily! As soon as one affirmation is complete or the goal has been reached, create another. Make affirmations a daily habit and soon you will not feel right unless you have done your daily practice. This will keep you focused in the direction of your dreams. Feel free to experiment with different oils as you progress.

Manufactured by Amazon.ca
Bolton, ON

14111691R00063

Angie Taylor is a Dr. of Natural Health who believes we've all lost sight of what real wellness feels like. As an Authentic Midwife, and International Board Certified Lactation Consultant, Angie discovered that the emotional state is what runs wellness. Angie became a Board Certified Holistic Alternative Psychology Master, Certified Aromatherapist, and Certified Aroma Freedom Technique Practitioner so that she could better serve her clients; knowing that clearing the body of negative emotional garbage would ultimately lead to total wellness in mind, body and spirit.

I love that life is a journey! More importantly it's a never ending adventure that takes us through twists and turns that stretch us further than we ever imagined. The things we have the opportunity to learn about ourselves on a daily basis is truly inspiring and, for far too many, frightening.

Aroma Freedom Technique, created by Dr. Benjamin Perkus, gives us all a way to truly enjoy the journey and look forward to every adventure that life throws our way. Using essential oils to quickly release limiting beliefs that have a root in past emotional events gives each one of us the real gift of unleashing the God-given purpose we have held deep inside since our moment of birth.

I created this Aroma Freedom Technique (AFT) Session & Affirmation Journal so you have a place to keep track of your journey and adventures. The very first page is where you can keep a running list of things you want to work on as it's highly satisfying to check off what we have accomplished. The remaining pages are for you to use as you take yourself through an AFT session followed by the affirmation and daily anchoring routine. When you're ready to move forward, simply turn the page and begin to fill in each area.

Are you ready to start your journey? Hang on for the adventure of a lifetime!!

ISBN 9781090797919